THE
MEADOWLANDS

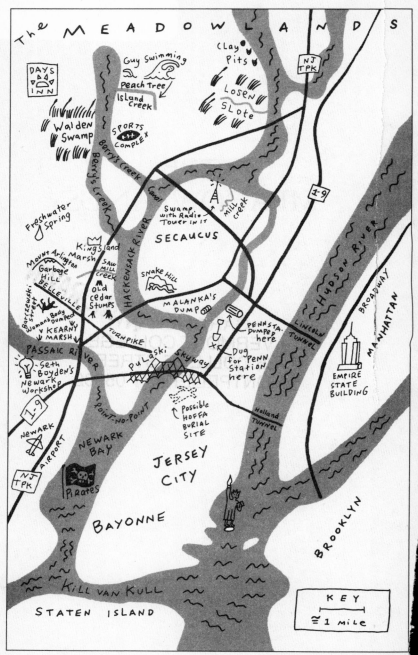

Designed by David Diehl 1998

THE
MEADOWLANDS

WILDERNESS ADVENTURES
AT THE EDGE OF A CITY

Robert Sullivan

ANCHOR BOOKS

Doubleday

New York London Toronto Sydney Auckland

AN ANCHOR BOOK
PUBLISHED BY DOUBLEDAY
a division of Random House, Inc.
1540 Broadway, New York, New York 10036

ANCHOR BOOKS, DOUBLEDAY, and the portrayal of an anchor are trademarks
of Doubleday, a division of Random House, Inc.

The Meadowlands was originally published in hardcover in 1998 by Scribner.
The Anchor Books edition is published by arrangement with Scribner.

Book design by Erich Hobbing

Library of Congress Cataloging-in-Publication Data

Sullivan, Robert, 1963–
The meadowlands : wilderness adventures at the edge of a city /
Robert Sullivan. — 1st Anchor Books ed.
p.   cm.
1. Hackensack Meadowlands (N.J.)—Description and travel.
2. Sullivan, Robert, 1963–   —Journeys—New Jersey—Hackensack
Meadowlands. I. Title.
[F142.H35S85   1999]
917.49'21—dc21   99-23159
                                                        CIP

ISBN 0-385-49508-0
Printed in the United States of America
First Anchor Books Edition: July 1999

3   5   7   9   10   8   6   4

For Suzanne

Contents

The world is charged with the grandeur of God.
    It will flame out, like shining from shook foil;
    It gathers to a greatness, like the ooze of oil
Crushed. Why do men then now not reck his rod?
Generations have trod, have trod, have trod;
    And all is seared with trade; bleared, smeared with toil;
    And wears man's smudge and shares man's smell: the soil
Is bare now, nor can foot feel, being shod.

And for all this, nature is never spent;
    There lives the dearest freshness deep down things;
And though the last lights off the black West went
    Oh, morning, at the brown brink eastward, springs—
Because the Holy Ghost over the bent
    World broods with warm breast and with ah! bright wings.

                    —"God's Grandeur"
                    by GERARD MANLEY HOPKINS, S.J.

   "I tell you one thing. If you dig out here, you sure as heck are
going to find something."

                    —AL McCLURE
                    animal control officer,
                    Health Department,
                    Secaucus, New Jersey

THE
MEADOWLANDS

Snake Hill

WHENEVER I'M IN NEW YORK AND I HAVE A LITTLE TIME ON my hands, I grab a backpack and some maps and a compass and maybe some lunch and I hike through Times Square and up the stairs of the Port Authority Bus Terminal, where I catch a bus out to the Meadowlands. The bus winds down the terminal's three-story ramp and dives into the mouth of the Lincoln Tunnel, which surrounds the bus with darkness and thick gray exhaust until it spits it out on the other side. As the cars around us scramble to be the first onto the highways of New Jersey, the bus struggles up the eastern side of Bergen Hill, while behind us the skyline of New York seems to shout at the bus's back and ask it where it's going. The leaves of the scraggly ailanthus trees wave in the wind of traffic as the bus passes through the cut in the red rocks that separate New York from New Jersey and the Meadowlands from the rest of the world. And then, in just a few minutes, as we drop down the other side of Bergen Hill and cruise into a low, flat land of lush grays and greens and pockets of rust and more and more circles of concrete, the bus seems to genuflect at the landscape before us. When the sky is clear, the water in the far-off creeks and rivers shines through the reeds like a sheet of aluminum foil that has been crumpled and then spread out again. When the sky is gray, the clouds mingle with the smokestacks' clouds of steam and smoke so that it is difficult to tell which is which.

After the bus courses down through cloverleafs, passing fields of cars waiting to pay tolls, turning onto smaller and smaller ramps and roads, and finally onto little local streets, I get out at the bus stop that is in a mall which was once an old cedar swamp, or at the stop in a grove of outlet stores, or maybe at the one in the center of Secaucus. The bus can be empty or it can be crowded with people who are on their way to the discount shopping outlets in the Meadowlands or to the giant sports and entertainment complex that is also known as the Meadowlands, or even to the little towns and cities along the edges of what remains of the old swamp. These people go to the Meadowlands for a deal on a dress or a pair of slacks or for a good time or to go home and have dinner and go to bed, while I go to the Meadowlands to explore. When I leave the bus, I will often head for the towns around the edges of the swamp or for ancient industrial sites that are now rusting and fading away. In the cars on the highways all around me, or in the planes that take off from Newark Airport, people have packed their trunks or their backpacks or their carry-on luggage with travel books or maybe brand-new water-repellent hiking clothes or PowerBars and polypropylene underwear, and they are heading West to travel and explore. But I am creeping slowly back into the East, back to America's *first* West—making a reverse commute to the already explored land that has become, through negligence, through exploitation, and through its own chaotic persistence, explorable again.

As often as not, when I head for the Meadowlands, I head for Snake Hill, which is a one-hundred-and-fifty-foot-tall rock that sticks up out of the very middle of the Meadowlands like a geological mistake. To get there I walk through downtown Secaucus, where I pass neat little homes and feel as if I startle each one. I pass some corporate headquarters and then warehouses and then a prison, at which point, with Snake Hill now before me, there is very little of anything left to pass at all.

At the base of Snake Hill, the leaves of aspen trees quiver nervously in the breeze of the Hackensack River. The landscape is like something out of Arizona or the South Dakota Badlands; in the summer, squadrons of dragonflies and mosquitoes patrol the dry land over waves of heat. On weekends, teenagers sometimes ride motorbikes around Snake Hill, darting among the trees and climbing up its quarried carcass—their engines sound like chain saws—but on weekdays, after I pass the guards at the prison, no one is around, and the only sounds are of the wind in the reeds, and the occasional freight or passenger train, and the constant rush of traffic on the New Jersey Turnpike. Altogether, the chorus is a kind of wild industrial New Jersey sound track, which, unlike the environmental sounds of the Eastern forests and Pacific Coast whale migration routes, is not available on cassette or CD. It takes another half an hour to climb the rocks to the top of Snake Hill. On the way up, I sneak through little dark forests and bushwhack through large wild fields of tall grass, both of which are nearly invisible from the highway. At the top, I can see for miles. To the north and west, a low ridge contains the area like a bowl with a lip made of little cities and towns. To the east, I can still see the Manhattan skyline, only now it is not shouting but whispering from behind another ridge. To the south, I can see out past the refineries and their towers of smoke and flame, out past the boat-loading cranes that feed along the cargo-containered fields of the Port of Newark like huge dark insects, out toward the Atlantic Ocean.

Before anyone ever stood on top of Snake Hill, the Meadowlands were a giant glacial lake that began receding in 8000 B.C. and still seems to be receding to this day. The glacier that cleared the way for what was eventually named Lake Hackensack was a mile thick, and it dumped boulders, rocks, clay, sand, and silt into what would have been a deep bay, so that before the Meadowlands even became the Meadowlands it was a field of haphazardly assembled debris. As the lake's cold freshwater drained off and seawater crept in, the bottom of the lake changed into a swamp and then a bog, and then a salt water marsh, and then, in some places, a kind of combination of all three. It was a giant inland estuary, a brackish place where microscopic organisms rose from a stew of decomposed plants and animals and other microscopic life, where the Hackensack River and the Passaic River were cleaned and purified and restocked with life—a hydrological kidney. When humans arrived in the Meadowlands, in about 10,000 B.C., and went from leaving huge piles of oyster shells to dumping increasingly poisonous waste, from homes, then from workshops, then from factories. At one point very recently in its history the Meadowlands was the largest garbage dump in the world.

At first, the Meadowlands were impervious to large-scale construction and development. The floor of muck and clay, in some places twenty stories deep, sucked down anything built upon it, and for every skyscraper raised up in Manhattan, one valley away, the Meadowlands swallowed another future city, another wondrous scheme. The Meadowlands stayed empty and wild, taunting progress. But soon engineers developed methods with which to build on the swamps. As New York City grew, it gazed over at the Meadowlands and licked its chops. In 1959, a *New York Times* editorial entitled "Requiem for the Meadows," was only saying what most people thought about this reviled land of burning garbage dumps, of polluted canals, of smokestacked factories, and impenetrable reeds. The Meadowlands was the nation's eyesore, the blight separating New York and America. The Meadowlands cried out to be developed. "The city and its environs are bursting at its seams," *The Times* wrote. "The Meadows must go."

Eventually, some factories were built, along with warehouses and the first superhighway and later housing and office developments that resembled Snake Hill—like outcroppings of metamorphic rock, and today, shopping malls and office complexes and future fun parks threaten to eat up even more of the old meadows every year. But many more plans were scrapped, and of those that were executed, almost a century's worth of buildings and factories and half-completed projects were left in the Meadowlands to rot—adding a layer of rust and concrete rubble and dead dreams to thousands of years of decomposed marsh grasses and all that the glacier left behind. Even where developments were successful, the swamp still seems to have some psychic power. In 1977, an architectural critic appraised a home and office development built in the Meadowlands as "a new kind of place, neither urban nor suburban." "It is not a real city," he added, "it is not a small town, but something strangely in between." The Meadowlands has physical power too. The new roads rarely stay smooth for long in the Meadowlands. They buckle and sink and eventually begin the long journey down into the depths of the old swamp.

*   *   *

Sometimes, I sit on the top of Snake Hill until dusk, and I spread out my maps and marvel.

I marvel that I am in the middle of a thirty-two-square-mile wilderness, part natural, part industrial, that is five miles from the Empire State Building and a little bit bigger than Manhattan.

I marvel that the land before me was called "a swampy, mosquito-infested jungle . . . where rusting auto bodies, demolition rubble, industrial oil slicks and cattails merge in unholy, stinking union" by the authors of a 1978 federal report, and that now it is a good place to see a black-crowned night heron or a pied-billed grebe or eighteen species of lady-bugs, even if some of the waters these creatures fly over can oftentimes be the color of antifreeze.

I marvel that on the edges of the Meadowlands there are places that are stuffed with people (some blocks in Union City have the highest population density in the United States) but that in the middle of the Meadowlands there are acres and acres of land where there aren't any people at all.

I marvel that some TV cameramen based in New York City consider the kingdom of Snake Hill to be the one place in the area where a cameraman can get a shot of an aquatic bird ris-ing off a seemingly bucolic stretch of water with the World Trade Center at its back (it's also possible in a cemetery in Queens, but not without getting gravestones in the shot).

I marvel that the land before me produces such smells as the nauseating sulfurous smell that I encounter on some stretches of the turnpike, the smell of lemon-scented Joy dishwashing detergent that emanates from somewhere in the area under the Newark Bay Bridge that was once covered with acres and acres of soft green salt marsh grass and now is covered with acres and acres of sun-sparkled, newly imported cars, or the crisp, stark scent of Titanium White oil paint that rises from the western end of the Pulaski Skyway.

I marvel that American diplomats supposedly once tried to find a way to avoid driving Leonid Brezhnev, then the leader of the Soviet Union, through the Meadowlands on his way from New York to Washington, D.C., because they were embarrassed about the area, but they couldn't find a way around the Meadowlands and it ended up being okay because he thought all the smokestacks and industry were terrific.

I marvel that soot from the swamp grass fires in the Meadowlands sometimes floats in clouds over the Palisades and the Hudson and even manages to reach New York City and that years ago the same trip was made by clouds of Meadowlands mosquitoes, which were considered some of the fiercest in the world.

I marvel that when Orson Welles broadcast "The War of the Worlds," in 1938, many of the people who lived near the Meadowlands and had tuned into the program late just assumed that the Martians had landed in the Meadowlands: it was the obvious place.

I marvel that the motion picture industry began in New Jersey before moving out to Hollywood, and that when early filmmakers made films that starred the West, they used shots of the Meadowlands as stand-ins for the prairies. (Coincidentally, the wind running through the old fields of green marsh grass—the kind of grass that was there before progress scared it away—used to sound like the wind on the prairie too.)

I marvel that the sky in the Meadowlands is, altitudinally speaking, like a wedding cake, with layers of airplane activity that includes airplanes from Teterboro Airport, Newark Airport, and even planes waiting in line to land at La Guardia and JFK—planes that cruise over the Meadowlands and look down on it as if it were a desert flatland just outside the huge forest of buildings in Manhattan.

I marvel that in 1956 a man set out in the fall to walk across the meadows that are now paved concrete from Elizabeth to Newark and that he didn't show up until the next spring, when his body was found in a creek.

I marvel that somewhere before me, either in the end zones of a football field or in garbage dumps that still burn, are buried more reputed underworld figures than perhaps anywhere in the world.

On top of Snake Hill, I am on mysterious ground that is not guidebooked and that reads like a dead language. I am where European landscape painters once set up their easels to paint the quiet tidal estuaries and old cedar swamps and where now commuters in their cars on their way from New Jersey and Pennsylvania to New York City attempt to avoid being run down by trucks that haul motel-room-sized sleeping compartments with silver silhouettes of naked women guarding their back wheels. On top of Snake Hill, I am in the middle of a place that the forces of progress have perennially targeted but have never managed to completely control, a place that people rush past on their way to the rest of America, a place they spit at with their exhaust pipes. There, with the sun burning through the smog and lighting up the reeds, with eight lanes of traffic providing backup, I sing the Meadowlands. I am the dot on the Meadowlands' exclamation point.

If Snake Hill is the most prominent geological characteristic of the Meadowlands, then Secaucus is the Meadowlands' most conspicuous address. Of all the municipalities with land in the Meadowlands—places such as Newark, Harrison, Kearny,

North Arlington, Lyndhurst, East Rutherford, Carlstadt, Wood-Ridge, Moonachie, Little Ferry, Teaneck, Teterboro, Leonia, Ridgefield, Ridgefield Park, North Bergen, and Jersey City—Secaucus is the only one completely surrounded by water. The Hackensack River carves the town's western border, and at its east are Penhorn Creek and Cromakill Creek, two sometimes stagnant streams that are linked by a storm-drain-like stretch of water in the places where they pass beneath a collection of highway intersections and overpasses and cloverleafs so intricate that a schematic diagram of them all looks like a cell undergoing mitosis that is out of control:

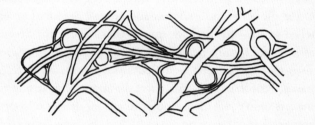

No one is certain about the origin of the name Secaucus. The place was originally listed as Siskakes in a Dutch deed to the land signed by Peter Stuyvesant, the governor of New Amsterdam, in 1658. Since then, Secaucus has been called Sickakus, Silkackes, Seacaucus, Cekakus, and Cecaicos, among other things. Big black snakes are said to have once inhabited the Secaucus environs—snake hunts were popular in the Meadowlands in the nineteenth century—and some say that the name Secaucus might have come from the Indian words *Sukit Achgook,* which mean black snake. Nicholas Fargnoli, the author of *The Minerals of Snake Hill,* speculated that other possible meanings of Secaucus are land of snakes, place of snakes, place where snakes hide, and land of terror.

Locally, the name Secaucus is pronounced *see-caw kiss,* with the accent on the first syllable and sometimes with a twinge of embarrassment. The embarrassment can be traced back to the First World War, when pig farming began to flourish in Secaucus. Each night, for nearly fifty years, trucks would fill up with swill from hotels and restaurants in Manhattan, which they would then dump in Secaucus's fields as feed for thousands of pigs. By one estimate, fifty million pounds of pork came out of Secaucus pig farms annually during the interwar years. The pig farms made the town a kind of joke that worked all over the country. People passing through the area in cars or on trains associated the stench with the pig farms, even though some of the other industries in and around Secaucus actually smelled worse—the garbage dumps that filled in the Secaucus meadows, for instance, or the rendering plants and slaughterhouses that discharged liquefied animal remains into local streams. People in Secaucus also talk about how at one time teenagers didn't like to visit other towns for dances or sporting events for fear of being ridiculed. When the New Jersey Turnpike was built across the Meadowlands in the 1950s, most of the pig farms moved or closed down, but they have only recently been forgotten. A few years ago, for instance, a boy brought an oyster shell to school that he had dug up in his backyard. The boy's teacher was not familiar with the most recent layer of geologic history in Secaucus, and the teacher examined the oyster carefully and announced to the class with great fanfare that the oyster the boy discovered in his backyard was perhaps as old as the last Ice Age. Old-timers in town knew that this oyster shell and the oyster that once called it home were more likely served up only a few decades ago at the Plaza Hotel or the Waldorf-Astoria or the Four Seasons or some other swanky place in New York City and that soon after it was dumped on a Secaucus pig farm not by a glacier but by a truck carrying a cargo of swill.

As the Meadowlands filled with trash and swill and rendering plants, Secaucus, like many towns in the Meadowlands, became concerned about its tarnished image. On several occasions, town leaders considered changing its name, to Clarendon or Laurel Manor. (Likewise, some people in town began to refer to Snake Hill as Laurel Hill.) As one Secaucus historian notes, "It was felt that 'Secaucus' made [the town] the butt of too many jokes which might possibly retard development." When name changes failed to stick, the town tied its hopes to development schemes, many of which never panned out. Just after World War II, for instance, Secaucus was chosen as the site for a huge private airport that was sponsored by Henry Berliner, an inventor who designed the Berliner, an extremely stable, parasol-type airplane that tested well with pilots—it was considered the first nonspinnable private plane—but saleswise never really took off. Berliner envisioned his Secaucus airport as the first of many that he assumed would be built as the United States experienced a huge boom in private air travel. The airport was to include a hotel, a restaurant, several hangars, and a shopping center, all housed in what was described as a series of futuristic interconnected steel-and-glass pavilions. A big hole was cut out of the meadows with Berliner's airport in mind (the hole was a mooring area intended to accommodate Howard Hughes's *Spruce Goose*), and that hole is visible from the air today, the only reminder of a big Meadowlands scheme that never got off the ground. Less grandiose developments did eventually come about, especially in the 1980s. Scores of outlet stores were built at that time as well as numerous hotels and movie theaters and some housing developments. All these buildings were bolted to the bedrock. In developing one formerly marshy area of town, Hartz Mountain, a major pet food company and Meadowlands development firm, drove so many steel girders into the ground that people joked Secaucus would become a new magnetic pole. Secaucus sought to tie its image to the sparkling new development, to make people forget about the pigs and the smell, but newcomers were wary. When a television station moved its base of operations from New York City to Secaucus, it avoided mentioning its new location until Secaucusites complained.

One day, when I took the bus to Secaucus, instead of hiking to Snake Hill, I hiked around downtown, where I hoped to learn more about Snake Hill and all the Meadowlands history it has seen. On that particular morning, the streets of Secaucus were filled with screaming emergency vehicles because while I had been riding the bus from New York two trains had crashed out in the Meadowlands and three people had died. The Meadowlands is notorious for train crashes. As far back as 1894, a fog on the meadows caused one train to rear-end another, killing eleven people, and in 1958, forty-eight people were killed when a train crashed through an open drawbridge and fell into Newark Bay in the worst commuter train accident in history. And whenever a train crashes, people are suddenly reminded of how wild and inaccessible the Meadowlands actually are. On the morning of the accident that happened when I was in town, the crash was so out of the way that rescue workers couldn't find it at first—a passenger with a cell phone had to describe the scene to a Secaucus emergency dispatcher who eventually figured out what part of the Meadowlands the passenger was calling from. The next day, news reports used terms like "windswept marshland" and "barren marshes," and illustrated their maps of the accident scene with the cartographer's symbol for swamp: ⚓ . One report said, "Though only three miles west of Manhattan, the site was strangely remote, a wintry marsh of scrub and frozen ponds, a mile from the nearest road . . ." I happened to speak with a fireman that morning as he was listening to the emergency radio frequency, and he told me that he overheard a helicopter pilot say that between the power lines and the swampy ground he couldn't find a place to land.

I made my way through the sirens to the little library in Secaucus. People were watching the crash coverage on TV, but I interrupted them to ask about Snake Hill. A librarian suggested I go across town and visit the Secaucus police garage, which is where Macy's used to store its Thanksgiving Day parade floats and is now the home of the Secaucus Museum. The museum's hours are by appointment only, but on that morning I was fortunate to run into Dan McDonough, a cheery-faced and animated man with a small silver mustache, who is Secaucus's historian. McDonough is also the editor and publisher of *Sports Reporter,* the oldest bowling newspaper in the nation, founded in 1940; a local photographer for twenty-nine years, who has photographed everything from weddings to class pictures to advertisements out of his studio in Jersey City; and an avid novice entomologist, who still collects black widow spiders in the Meadowlands from time to time, puts them in a climate-controlled receptacle marked CAUTION: DEADLY SPIDERS, and then brings them to the Museum of Natural History, in New York, where they are devenomed for scientific purposes. "They put little electrodes on their butts and squeeze out the venom," he told me.

As it happens, McDonough's knowledge of Secaucus history is Snake Hill oriented, so the Secaucus Museum is actually a kind of Snake Hill shrine. It features old photographs and newspaper clippings of Snake Hill when it was bigger than it is now (fifty feet taller, in fact, and five times as wide); of when it was decked out with lawns and gardens and the mansion-like buildings of various state institutions; of when Snake Hill was the site of, at different times, an almshouse, three separate churches, a children's eye hospital, and a penitentiary where prisoners in black-and-white-striped suits worked in gangs and split rocks on the hill. McDonough prides himself on being one of the few people in Secaucus to have a button that was once worn on the uniforms of the guards who worked on Snake Hill in the long-ago time when it was home to a psychiatric hospital—the button says "Lunatic Asylum." In the Secaucus Museum that day, McDonough recounted the story for me of how an ad executive named Mortimer Remington of J. Walter Thompson passed Snake Hill on a train trip from New York to Newark, and was inspired to create the Prudential Insurance Company's Rock of Gibraltar logo. And he told me that Hudson County hired a demolitions company to take Snake Hill away in 1962. It was to be leveled to a height of three feet. Today, a good portion of the hill is gone. It is often said that the only reason any of Snake Hill is still around is that the demolition company was afraid that blowing up the last bit of the hill might cause the turnpike bridge that runs alongside it to loosen or fall down. Sometimes, local residents refer to the black jagged ridge that remains as a rotten tooth.

When I asked McDonough why Snake Hill was ordered to be removed, he recommended I speak with his boss, the mayor of Secaucus. In the meantime, McDonough offered to give me a ride in his shiny blue Cadillac up across the meadows to Kearny. It was a cold, clear day. In a minute we were on the New Jersey Turnpike and we could see the train wreck off in the distance: the wounded silver locomotives, the red fire trucks, the buzz of emergency personnel activity in the calm sea of tall brown swamp grass. Just past the train wreck, McDonough pointed out a freshwater pond said to be good for catching bass. Then, we climbed higher over the Hackensack River, past some old Secaucus dumps and the graffitied remains of Snake Hill. And then we came down slowly on the other side of the Meadowlands, into the valley of dormant and active dumps, of abandoned junkyards and anonymous factories and more and more reeds. The reeds reminded McDonough of insects. "If you come back in the summer, it's all monarch butterflies," he said. "You can't believe it. You can pick 'em like berries in the meadows, five or six at a time. We put about forty monarch butterflies in the back of the car one time and then we drove up to my sister's house and she videotaped us letting them go. It was beautiful."

A few days after McDonough dropped me off, I met with Mayor Anthony Just. Mayor Just is a kind-faced man, with strong hands; he is robust for seventy-one years of age. In his office he keeps a photo of a fiery red sunset taken near Snake Hill, where he occasionally goes for lunch. He also keeps in his office a huge chunk of the hill itself. He was born and raised in Secaucus, and one of his two sons still lives in town, where he has a chiropractic practice. In front of his son's house, a few blocks from city hall, there is a sign:

A. JUST
CHIROPRACTOR

Mayor Just grew up on a pig farm. "Yes, Secaucus had the reputation for pigs," he said, "but I polish that reputation, and here's how I do it. I estimate there would be about two hundred thousand hogs a year at two hundred and fifty pounds per hog. That's fifty million pounds of pork per year. And now, what did we feed them anyway?" Mayor Just leaned back in his chair, as if he had just clinched an argument, and he pointed his finger at me. *"What you and I didn't eat!"* he went on. "The bakeries' day-old stuff, all that stuff from hotels in New York—we fed it to the pigs. So we were *recycling!* And we were recycling long before anybody else was." Mayor Just also remembers that farmers would wash swill off their fields with fire hoses and that the adjacent meadows in turn became sopped with swill and manure. (Years ago, a boy fell into a manure-filled marsh in Secaucus and drowned.) On the day I was in his office, Mayor Just was reminiscing about hardships on the pig farm, and he recalled that when one of his brothers went to war and there was no one of legal age to drive the swill truck in and out of New York, Mayor Just, then fifteen, used the birth certificate of another brother, Dominic, who had died as a child. In telling this story, Mayor Just became overwhelmed with emotion, and it was quiet for a long time in his office, except for the radio, which was playing a song by the Doobie Brothers. The silence was awkward for me after a while; I didn't know what to do. Finally, when he regained his composure, Mayor Just said, "I'm sorry. To me pig farms weren't a joke. They were like Norman Rockwell."

Among politicians, Mayor Just is known in the Meadowlands for opposing a project called Allied Junction, which would put five forty-story office towers on the old dumps and marshland next to Snake Hill. The mayor believes that the developers might better spend their time investing their money in the cities in the area—Newark and Jersey City, for example—than in swampland. He also opposes building residential housing near Snake Hill. "Back there they buried fifty-five-gallon drums of everything," he said. "I say if you put housing in there you will create another one of those Love Canal situations." In general, he believes that despite all the environmental regulations that have been put in place over the years, and despite public awareness of the ecological value of wetlands, the Meadowlands are still dumped on, literally and figuratively, and that Secaucus is dumped on in particular. To prove his point, he cites a recent government cleanup project in which toxic soil was dug up in Kearny and then redumped in Secaucus. His opponents say he wants to return to the days of the pig farms, but he vehemently denies this. "If you ask me, the government should do something to save that area," he said. "Not that it's a forest or anything. But it's a forest in another way. You know what I'd like to accomplish up there on Snake Hill? I'd like to see a big flagpole up there, because to me, it's the biggest point in the area."

The thought of a lone flag flying from the denuded peak of Snake Hill prompted the mayor to reflect for a moment. He sat back thoughtfully and squeezed the arms of his office chair as he gazed at the piece of Snake Hill sitting next to the little toy pig collection he keeps on top of a coffee table. After a while, he said, "You know what it is? It's that people around here don't venture out anymore. What I used to find interesting was I would park my car out where the jail is now, right near Snake Hill, and I would just walk. One day I went out there on Mother's Day after dinner. I remember it was Mother's Day because I was all dressed up and I thought, What am I doing here on Mother's Day? The answer was I was on one of my adventures. And you know, I was always angry about Snake Hill's big demolition. That was John V. Kenny who ordered that. He was the big Hudson County boss, and they said he was angry with us for not putting a racetrack here.

We voted against it, so they said, 'Let's take down their Snake Hill.' When I was walking along and looking at the sunset and the hill, I would say, 'Rot in hell, John V. Kenny, for destroying this piece of God's creation!' And you know, once when I was back there I called the cops because I found a skull. In fact, I would bet you find a lot of human remains back there. I would bet a dinner on it, because they used to have an old graveyard back there, and when they moved it for the turnpike, they just moved it all at once with a backhoe. In fact, when I found that skull, I started to take it, but then I took it back. I figure everybody deserves someplace."

A call came through around then. Mayor Just asked his secretary to take a message.

"But this time on Mother's Day," he continued, "I was walking along and I found some of these pieces of Snake Hill that they had blasted off, and I put them in some pails. So then there I am—walking along the tracks with the pails and these rocks in them. I remember thinking that if I had a heart attack then my political opposition were going to say, 'Look! See! He *was* crazy! He's got two buckets of rocks!' " The mayor leaned forward in his chair and smiled. "You see," he said, "they wouldn't have known the significance of the rocks."

My own explorations in the Meadowlands began when I was in high school. I would cross the area with friends in someone's parents' car while we were on our way to New York City from New Jersey to see rock concerts or sporting events or other things that brought teenagers from New Jersey into New York. Sometimes, while crossing—usually on the return trip— we would take a wrong exit off the turnpike and ride down into a swampy deserted area or try an old road looking for a shortcut, and in any case have no idea where we were. As a result, we would often come home late, and sometimes get into trouble. Later, after college, I worked for a newspaper in New Jersey, and occasionally I would be sent to the fringes of the Meadowlands, where I could look out at the smokestacks and bridges and see acres and acres of reeds and wonder what they were all about. When I moved to New York City and got married, I experienced the Meadowlands as a pastime—visiting them once in a while with a friend who wanted to test out his new four-wheel-drive car or taking my wife there to see an old bridge, but mostly just reading little bits about them in newspapers or staring down into them from a bus or a car or a train.

A few years ago, I moved away from New York and I realized that the Meadowlands had been like a bad habit for me and now that I was away from them I needed a bigger fix. I would walk into the woods outside of the city where I ended up living and see beautiful trees and huge mountains topped with spectacular glaciers that altogether only made me miss the world's greatest industrial swamp. When this happened, I began taking cross-country trips to the Meadowlands and spending more and more time there. I also began making more intensive surveys of the area, and the Meadowlands turned out to be a lot bigger than I thought. I hiked and I walked and I rented cars and in the end I figure I covered close to three thousand miles in rental cars alone—there's no telling how many miles I was driven by other people. In the process of hiking and canoeing and digging and just otherwise exploring the area, I learned a lot about what happens inside old mountains of trash, about all of the inventions that were invented in the Meadowlands, about a great mosquito trapper, about people who enjoy spending as much time in the Meadowlands as possible, about a lot of old crimes.

At first, it seemed enough just to go through the Meadowlands on the usual made-for-humans routes, but after a while I became preoccupied with seeing the things on my maps that I couldn't see from a car. In the Meadowlands, there are a lot of places that require a kind of all-terrain vehicle that has yet to be built, and so I soon found myself buying more sophisticated exploration equipment, such as a boat. Meanwhile, I prepared to explore the other Meadowlands—the Meadowlands that is underground—with shovels and picks and metal detectors and whatever else I could get my hands on. I searched for the dumped ruins of world cities, and on one occasion, I attempted to excavate the most famous of all the bodies said to be dumped in the Meadowlands, the body of Jimmy Hoffa. On many of these trips, I was accompanied by my friend Dave. Dave is my best friend from high school. He is also the great-great-great-great-great-nephew of Meriwether Lewis, or something like that—his mother is the only one who can explain it. Together, Dave and I mounted several expeditions into the quasi-natural heart of the Meadowlands—the kinds of places that Dave's great-great-great-great-great-uncle had at his back when he and Clark took off to explore, the kinds of places where, if you have ever seen them, you might not want to go.

On all my trips, I found that I was greeted warmly by the citizens of the Meadowlands and its environs, even if my enthusiasm for their region was often regarded initially with disbelief. On one of my first official forays into the Meadowlands a few years ago, when I was walking through Secaucus toward a little stream called Mill Creek, I stopped to spread my maps out on the street in an attempt to identify a particular swamp with a radio tower in it. Suddenly, a man came running out of his home, one of many built right up to the edge of the swamp. He said, "You're not lost in Secaucus, are you?"

We talked awhile, and he told me that he was an accountant who was born in Secaucus and who was unemployed at the moment and had recently returned from Japan, where he hoped to pick up the Japanese language and Japanese accounting contacts. After a while, I asked him if he knew the name of the swamp with the radio tower in it. He nodded his head. "Yes," he said. "In Secaucus, we refer to that as the swamp with the radio tower in it."

I thanked him and folded up my maps and continued on, because at that point I still had a lot of ground to cover.

An Achievement
of the Future

FROM A CAR STUCK IN TRAFFIC ON THE WAY TO A GIANTS
game, or in a train as it races past scum-covered puddles and
dormant dumps, one might think the name Meadowlands as
applied to the area is a joke, but once it was perfectly apt.
Once, there were actual meadows in the Meadowlands, decorated with wildflowers the way they are today littered with
bits of paper and plastic and truck tire shards. In the spring of
1819, John Torrey, the father of American botany, toured the
Jersey meadows and reported patches of white, yellow, and
purple violets. In other springs around that time, there was
yellow floating arum, blue veronica, and white saxifrage. In
summers, botanists reported seeing blue iris, pink mead-
owsweet, pink marshmallow, pale purple wild hibiscus, white
ladies' tresses, purple snake's mouth, and green and purple

orchids. In the fall, there were yellow goldenrod, bright red cranberries, and the tops of the cattails turned a dark, burned-out-looking brown, anticipating future area land uses. Up until 1910, when an oil spill wiped the plant out completely, wild rice grew on the banks of the creeks in the Meadowlands. Back in 1819, Torrey wrapped up his report by noting, "much remains to be discovered."

The local Indian tribes were the first people known to have given a name to the Meadowlands. The area was used by many different tribes as seasonal fishing and hunting grounds, but it was inhabited by a tribe often referred to as the Hackensacks. They were a branch of the Lanapes, who disappeared from the Meadowlands by 1750, because of disease, the development of British- and Dutch-style farms, and massacres led by settlers in New York. The Hackensacks probably lived on a ridge overlooking the meadows that still surround Overpeck Creek, where today they would have a good view of the Vince Lombardi Rest Area on the New Jersey Turnpike. The names of some of their Sachems were Wawapehack, Wewenatokwee, Kogkhennigh, Memiwokan, Therinques, and Sames. The first European settlers of the Meadowlands heard the meadows in the area of Newark referred to as *Mankachkewachky,* which they took to mean *the great marsh.* The meadows between the Passaic and the Hackensack Rivers were called *Meghgectecock,* but I couldn't find the definition of this word listed anywhere. Other words that the Hackensacks might have used to describe all or parts of the Meadowlands included *Maskek,* which meant swamp; *Schingaskunk,* which meant bog meadow; *Awonn,* which meant fog or mist; *Maskequimin,* which meant swamp huckleberry; *Pulpecat,* which was the word for deep dead water; and *Eike!* which meant wonderful. Some of the first white settlers in the Meadowlands were British merchants who emigrated from Barbados, so for a long time during the 1700s, the Meadowlands were known as New Barbadoes.

The number of animal species on hand for the first Meadowlands settlers was comparable to the number of cars on the turnpike on a Friday night before a holiday. Wild turkeys lived on the edges of the marshes, along with plovers, partridges, wood and water snipes, pheasants, heath hens, cranes, herons, bitterns, quail, merlins, thrushes, and scores of songbirds. Bald eagles, falcons, and numerous species of hawks circled the huge Meadowlands sky. In salt water that by 1970 would be nearly incapable of supporting life, Indians fished for codfish, weakfish, herring, mackerel, thornbacks, flounders, plaice, sheepsheads, and blackfish. In freshwater they fished for salmon, striped bass, drumfish, shad, carp, perch, pike, trout, roach, sturgeon, bullheads, suckers, sunfish, eels, and lampreys. On islands in the marshes, there were elk, deer, wolves, beavers, mink, otters, fishers, catamounts, hares, martens, flying squirrels, bears, and mountain lions. Huge flocks of red-winged blackbirds and passenger pigeons flew through the skies of the Meadowlands. Residents caught the passenger pigeons and ate them after fattening them for a few days. The residents said that the pigeons tasted like chicken.

There was so much meadow in the Meadowlands that the first landowners gave it away free to incoming citizens who had purchased land higher up in the valley, as if the meadows were something in a Welcome Wagon kit. Technically, the grass that covered the Meadowlands was spartina but it was called salt hay. The short coarse salt hay was considered worthless. "Horses do not like this hay, and the milk of cows eating it rapidly sours," one farmer wrote. The horses liked the other hay, which was called *Juncus bulbosus* and covered the areas in Newark where junkyards are today. (*Juncus bulbosus* is now known as *J. gerardi* or black rush, and it exists only in a few areas, having mostly been choked out by *Phragmites communis,* the tall and ubiquitous swamp grass that thrives in ecologically distressed areas all over the world.) Hay farmers cut the salt hay twice a year, stacked it in heaps, and waited until the ground was frozen to collect the stacks. When walking on the meadows, horses wore special wooden shoes and farmers' feet froze. During the summer, both horses and farmers risked being ravaged by mosquitoes, and there was always the threat of being duped by other farmers. The stakes that marked each farmer's land were easily moved or replaced, and when winter came the farmers practiced what could be considered a kind of reverse illegal dumping, harvesting the stack most convenient to their cart. In 1805, Newark had to hire a salt marsh manager to keep order on the marshes. "[I]t is said of our forefathers . . . that they are mostly unscrupulous," a Newark-area historian reported in 1908. In the 1890s, when bananas were first shipped into America, salt hay was used to store bananas in the numerous banana houses that popped up on the Meadowlands at the time. Salt hay was also used in stables, in ice-houses, in brick making, in glass and crockery factories, and later to make asphalt and coffin mattreses. In the fall of 1958, Bill Ballenski, a second-generation Newark hay farmer who was thought to be the last in the area, stopped farming after thirty-seven years. He was getting thirty-six dollars a ton.

Aside from salt hay, farmers utilized all different parts of the old meadows. They used the cattail and blue-bent for thatching and caning chairs, which were then sold in New York. In the late 1800s, a man named John L. Earle was known for stripping eight hundred pounds of cattails in one day. Daniel Van Winkle, the president of the Hudson County Historical Society in the 1920s, once recalled that young people in the Meadowlands used to spend winter days making lanterns by filling clam shells with lard and adding a bit of cotton cloth; when the lanterns were lit, they filled homes along the edge of the swamp with what Van Winkle remembered as "a dim and flickering light." The clay that lies beneath everything in the Meadowlands made for a vibrant brick-making industry from 1870 until the 1950s. At its peak, in 1895, the brickyards in Little Ferry produced one hundred million bricks, which were used to make buildings in Newark, Paterson, New York City, and Providence, Rhode Island. The use of steel in building construction eventually closed the brickyards down and the clay pits filled with water so that they began to look like ponds. Now the pits are fenced off, but a woman in Little Ferry told me that until a few years ago children went swimming in the holes. The water was ice cold and just about every summer someone would drown.

The most tantalizing former natural feature of the Meadowlands are the cedar forests. A cedar forest covered a stretch of land as big as midtown Manhattan in Kearny, and a forest ran across the desertlike area where the Meadowlands Sports Complex is today. It is estimated that cedars once covered between a third and a half of the Meadowlands. They grew in dense, dark stands. They were forty to sixty feet tall and lived to be two hundred years old. The wood from the white cedar tree was soft but straight-grained and durable and not easily burned. It was used extensively in boat building and in the manufacture of shingles, which were sold locally, in New York, and in the West Indies, where there was also a robust market for pickled Newark Bay oysters. A number of people made a living as lumbermen in the Meadowlands, though it wasn't long before the cutting of the cedars went too far. Peter Kalm, a Swedish naturalist who toured the Meadowlands in 1750, wrote, "The inhabitants here are not only lessening the number of their trees, but are even expatriating them entirely. . . . By these means many swamps are already quite destitute of cedars." There was a period close to the time of the Revolutionary War when a second growth of cedars briefly recharged the local lumber industry—in 1776, the Continental Army floated cedar logs cut from the Meadowlands in New York Harbor in an effort to disrupt British shipping—but surveys of the area made soon after tell of the former existence of the Meadowlands' forest with a dose of modern disbelief and awe.

Even without cutting, the cedars probably would have died. The Hackensack was dammed upstream in 1902, increasing the salt water content in the Meadowlands. Meanwhile, the meadows were catching on fire more often; hay farming was dying out (salt hay sales to stables dropped with the advent of the car), and the uncut grass was more likely to burn. By 1937, there was only one patch of cedar forest left in Moonachie, near where Donna Karan, the fashion designer, now has a big office. The stumps of the cedar forests remain in the Meadowlands today, and you can see them from the highways and railroads at low tide. They look like piles of old bones. Recently, a dentist on the Turnpike Commission complained that they were an eyesore, but his term expired before anyone had a chance to yank them out.

There is a spring that trickles up out of the ground in the Meadowlands. It bubbles with cold, fresh water that has tested pure. The spring is in an area zoned industrial on the North Arlington meadows, and if you stand in the spring's little pond of cold water and turn west, your eyes meet the face of a one-hundred-foot-tall red sandstone cliff. The cliff is part of an eight-mile-long ridge that contains the Meadow-lands on the west. When the sky pours down rain, little waterfalls fall off the top of the cliff here and there, so that if you make a fake telescope with your hands and block out the backyards on the top of the cliff and you concentrate on the little leafy trees instead of the garbage dumps behind you, then you can imagine you're in a tropical place. If your fake telescope has an X-ray function, then you can see through the ridge to the caves and holes and tunnels inside, which are the remains of the Schuyler mine, the first successful mine in America. It was begun in 1715 by Arent Schuyler, a merchant of Dutch descent from Albany, New York, who moved to the Meadowlands to be closer to his third wife's family in Manhattan. Schuyler's estate on the Meadowlands was called Schuyler's Plantation, and it included a mansion built with bricks from Holland, formal gardens, and a fenced-in park area where he kept and hunted deer. Schuyler owned approximately two hundred slaves, and it is said that in 1714, one of those slaves uncovered a green rock on the grounds of the plantation, a rock that was later determined to contain copper. This find precipitated the industrial revolution in America. It also precipitated America's first gold rush, which occured in the Newark area. When people heard about the copper find, they began hunting for other rocks. In a letter to the British Crown written at the time, the governor of what was then called East Jersey wrote, "[T]here must be a great allowance made for the humour that now prevails to run a mine-hunting."

The Schuyler mine was the site of America's first mine shaft, the Victoria Shaft, which was sunk to a depth of approximately one hundred feet in the 1730s and was initially a success but then filled with water. When Arent Schuyler died, his eldest son, Colonel John Schuyler, took over management of the mine, and when he did he decided, at the urging of Benjamin Franklin, to import a steam engine from England that would power a water pump. The steam engine arrived in September 1753, along with crates and crates of spare parts and its designer and operator, Josiah Hornblower. Hornblower spent a year building the engine. When he finally fired it up, the contraption looked like a giant chicken drinking water— its beak nudged by the steam engine, its tail activating the water pump. People came from all over the world to see the mine and its engine on the edge of the meadows, risking mosquitoes and bad roads. A member of a German scientific society praised the effort, while a French group said it was a good mine but that the English design was all wrong. The pump was destroyed in a fire in 1768, and the mine was eventually shut down. The site was reopened on several occasions, though not always as a mine. In the 1850s, a stash of silverware, apparently stolen from homes in Newark, was found in one of the shafts. In 1923, mushrooms grown in the mines won second place at the National Mushroom Growers Fair in Washington, D.C. In 1926, a group of radio enthusiasts tested whether the mine improved radio reception (it didn't).

In 1933, the tunnel was mapped by a sixteen-year-old explorer. He drew long thin tunnels and giant scooped-out caves, with names such as Devil's Head, the X-Way, Convict's Bedroom, and Tunnel of Death. Around the same time, mothers in the area complained enough to have it closed, but that didn't stop other young explorers. In 1949, the Newark *Star-Ledger* reported, "Police discovered that the youngsters were using the damp, narrow streets as a playground." When the mine was closed this time, the police used dynamite to seal it shut. Kids still found ways in, but mostly people in the area forgot about the mine. Then, on the morning of November 30,

1989, a distressed homeowner called North Arlington's city hall to say that there was a huge hole opening up in his backyard. Soon, more homeowners were calling with similar reports, and people began to wonder if North Arlington was being swallowed up entirely. In one case, a hole twenty feet deep gulped down a pine tree. The next day, North Arlington was swarming with TV cameras. Geologists arrived by helicopter. Radar showed approximately four dozen holes. Nobody knew what caused them until someone overlaid a map of the mysterious holes on top of an old map of the Schuyler mine covered with little dots that represented shafts. The dots matched. A building called the Schuyler Condominiums was on top of two old mine shafts. The city plugged the holes with concrete, and everything seems to have settled now, but city officials continue to monitor ground movement to this day.

The synergy between industry and the Meadowlands continued long after the steam engine was introduced to America on behalf of the Schuyler mine—though nowhere more perfectly than in Newark, the Meadowlands capital city. In 1666, Robert Treat, the leader of a group of Puritans from Connecticut, founded Newark. He did not have industry in mind; he chose the site for the seclusion the Meadowlands offered. But at the beginning of the nineteenth century, Newark's isolation was the impetus for its quick and ferocious industrialization. In 1800, with no hope for a great port in the Meadowlands' shallow water, the commerical interests in Newark promoted local crafts and artisans. The promotion worked. In 1801, twelve hundred people, most of them farmers, lived in Newark; a French visitor at the time called Newark "the most beautiful village on the continent." Sixty years later, three-fourths of Newark's population worked in industry, and Newark had become the largest industrially based city in the country. Newark's industry began with shoes. In 1806, one third of all Newarkers made shoes of one kind or another, including the tennis shoe, which was developed by a local businessman named Thomas Cort. Shoe businesses moved to New England after the Civil War, but Newark kept its tanneries and developed the first Russian leather, the first great quantities of Morrocan leather, and the first leather made from alligators and other reptiles. Just as Newark's shoes had been worn by models in Paris, so too was its leather prized: the Emperor William of Germany sent to Newark for the leather that he used to decorate the interior of his carriage. Leather was tanned by soaking animal hides in vats of dung after men scraped out the flesh from the hides with their bare hands. The by-products of leather making, like the by-products of all of Newark's new industrial processes, were flushed out through the creeks and streams and into the meadows. The Newark poor suffered the most for this because the poorhouse was built on the edge of the polluted and malarial swamp, but everyone else in Newark suffered too: today, public health historians know Newark in the 1860s as the unhealthiest city in America.

Tradespeople who migrated to Newark to work in its factories brought manufacturing ideas with them, and Newark became a nineteenth-century equivalent of Silicon Valley, a hotbed of invention. The motion picture industry's birth in Newark was thanks to the Reverend Hannibal Goodwin, a local pastor, who had been searching for a material he could use to make unbreakable stereoscopic slides of Bible scenes when he came up with an early plastic film. (His discovery was marked by an explosion in his parsonage.) The plastics industry thrived in Newark. In 1868, when world elephant herds had dwindled enough to cause a severe ivory pool ball shortage in the United States, a pool ball manufacturer offered ten thousand dollars to anyone who could develop an ivory substitute. John Wesley Hyatt, a typesetter in Albany, New York, worked with another typesetter, James Brown, and mixed ordinary cotton and acids and camphor to create a hard, pinkish clot of what his brother, Isaiah, later named celluloid. In 1873, Hyatt took his share of the prize money and moved to Newark, where he perfected his invention. In just a few years, Hyatt's celluloid was everywhere. It was used to make knife handles, hair ornaments, horse harness buckles, button, combs, brush handles, and artificial teeth. Celluloid collars replaced men's paper shirt collars, and instead of washing the shirts, people just removed the collar, wiped it with a cloth, and replaced it, prolonging by several days the length of time men felt they could wear their shirts without having them cleaned. Toys were made with celluloid, including the Kewpie doll and the first doll that said "Mama." The return top was invented in Newark by Charles Kirchof, a German immigrant. He had been trained to be a surgeon, but the sight of blood repulsed him so he turned to engineering instead. He left Germany during a revolution in 1848 just before he was to be shot by a firing squad, and fled to New York where he invented a stock ticker for the blind. The return top was only successful years later when it was renamed the yo-yo. As plastics increased in popularity, John Wesley Hyatt went on to invent methods of molding plastic and eventually perfected the plastic ball bearing. He then invented a kind of sugarcane mill, a sewing machine, a method of solidifying hardwood to produce golf club heads, mallets, and bowling balls. In the meantime, a problem developed with the collars and ornamental hair combs and other things that were made with the celluloid. They began to explode. People died when their hair combs caught fire, when their shirt collars burst into flames. The recipe was successfully adjusted, however, and the new improved celluloid was used, redemptively, in 1921, to make the first automobile safety glass.

The greatest inventor ever to live in Newark, Seth Boyden, was also one of the greatest American inventors. Boyden was born in Massachusetts, where as a young boy he invented several different kinds of microscopes and telescopes. In 1818, shortly after he first arrived in Newark, he invented a machine to strip leather, which, combined with a method of varnishing that he subsequently devised, made patent leather. He got the idea after admiring the bill of a German military officer's cap. After he invented patent leather, he had it patented and he gave the patent away. This was characteristic of how he handled the patents on most of his inventions. When he was thirty-seven, for instance, he figured out how to make malleable steel, and in so doing founded the modern steel industry. He made malleable steel by adding pit or rosin to the coal that heated the metal—he got this idea from watching a blacksmith's fire as a boy. He announced the invention on July 4, 1826, and immediately sold his steel business and set about something else. At night, Boyden kept a notepad by his bed that was rigged with wires that guided his hand horizontally and enabled him to write in the dark. He was often seen on the streetcars in Newark sketching or making notes or muttering to himself. At one point, he had a friend who was attempting to court women in Newark, and his friend felt that his gray hair was holding him back, so Boyden invented a hair dye. Boyden wore the hair dye downtown to test it. On the first few days, Boyden's hair was jet-black. Then his hair was green, and later it turned purple. After hurting one of his eyes, Boyden invented a U-shaped lens that allowed him to look at his bad eye with his good one.

In the course of his life in Newark, Boyden built the first locomotives in the United States and then built some more in Cuba. He invented the boxcar; a way to refine zinc; a method of drawing electricity from the earth with cotton. He invented the first American daguerreotype after reading in a magazine about a process developed by Louis Daguerre in France. (Samuel Morse heard about his daguerreotype and came to see it, and then got to know Boyden, who later helped Morse smooth out difficulties with the telegraph.) Boyden also invented an air gun, a rifle, an electric clock, an electric garden fountain, an electric barometer that could predict a storm eighty-six hours in advance, and a kind of imitation gold, which irked gold retailers in the Newark area. In 1849, he went to California with his son Obadiah during the Gold Rush. He kept a journal so detailed that your eyes glaze over when you read it. When he came back to Newark, a little more than a year later, the city fired a cannon in his honor. Despite all his inventions, Boyden was poor in the last years of his life. A group of local businessmen gave him use of a farm on the outskirts of Newark where he became obsessed with growing strawberries. He was convinced that he could grow a strawberry the size of a pineapple and managed to grow one that weighed fifteen pounds. For many years after his death, there was a parade in Newark on his birthday, but after a while no one bothered. It's as if Boyden invented so many things that were taken for granted that he was eventually taken for granted too.

One day I drove across the Meadowlands to Newark to find Seth Boyden's grave. I drove along old broad streets of once impressive buildings that now housed cheap electronics stores. I passed abandoned and boarded-up buildings and abandoned public housing towers and vacant lots, and then some modern skyscrapers filled with law firms' offices and decorated with fountains and security guards. I drove up along the Passaic River and I could see over to Harrison and Kearny, which were once meadows and then became homes to huge factories that had developed cables and electronic devices and all the communication equipment for the entire East Coast and now seem in places to be in the process of becoming some kind of meadow again. Finally, I came to the great stone gate of the Mount Pleasant Cemetery. I saw only the caretaker, who directed me to Seth Boyden's grave. It was decorated with a simple obelisk. The caretaker directed me to the gravestone of Henry Herbert, a writer who lived in a house overlooking the cemetery and who wrote under the pen name Frank Forestor and was one of the first editors of the *Atlantic Monthly.* The caretaker told me that Herbert became despondent when his wife died and his children were sent to live in Europe; he said that in 1858 when Herbert threw himself a party to cheer himself up and no one came, Herbert killed himself. After walking around the cemetery a little longer, I got in the car, drove back to Newark, and went to the Newark Public Library to read more about Seth Boyden and all that he had made. There, at a computer terminal, I saw a man printing out a list of books under the subject heading Wind Power. He looked to be in his fifties and in his lap he had a patent directory for inventors.

People were always trying to invent new uses for the Meadowlands; most people felt *anything* was better than what was there. In an article written in 1899 entitled "An Achievement of the Future," Charles J. McGillycuddy wrote, "Within three miles of the New York City Hall is a tract of wasteland, seventy-two square miles in extent. Its reclamation and utilization is an achievement of the near future which will prove an object lesson to every community in the United States." McGillycuddy went on to call the area "the result of an incredible lack of enterprise in the most enterprising and progressive country in the world." For McGillycuddy, the Meadowlands spat in the face of progress. A few years before McGillycuddy made these observations, Cornelius C. Vermeule had said many of the same things. Aside from being the state geologist, Vermeule was an internationally known sanitary engineer, and in 1896 he wrote the first of several long reports on the advantages of developing the Meadowlands. Vermeule considered the meadows not only an eyesore but a health hazard—at conferences he showed deaths from fevers and disease to be 50 percent more numerous for the half of the population of New Jersey who lived near swamps than for the rest of the state's residents. To replace the wasteland, he proposed a kind of futuristic theme park, an industrial city with one-hundred-foot-wide canals, where waste was funneled through in sewers resembling arteries. The Meadowlands in their existing state were repugnant to Vermeule, but he at least allowed that some people might have reason to appreciate them. "[O]nly those with a highly artistic sense, and the ability to forget the evil sanitary influences lurking beneath the waving reeds and grasses, can appreciate these beauties," he wrote.

Vermeule's plan was never enacted, and in time other grand and similarly unenacted plans took its place. In the 1930s, for instance, a plan to develop the Meadowlands would have straightened the Hackensack River, a stream that suffered from what one report termed "excessive sinuosities, which handicapped the industrial development of the area."

In 1958, a group of art students at Pratt Institute in Brooklyn, New York, drew up plans for what was described as "a fabulous city powered by atomic energy with a population of 600,000 enjoying a new pattern of life . . ."; when a reporter asked the Pratt professor why the Meadowlands were chosen as the site of this proposed city of monorails and moving sidewalks, he responded: "It was a challenge. You know, it's phenomenal—here you have 30,000 barren acres in the middle of the densest metropolitan area in the world." A dam across the river just above the beginning of Newark Bay was proposed by several people, including J. J. van Wouw and R. Tutein Nolthehius, two engineers brought by developers to New Jersey from the Netherlands. (Meadowlands developers have historically sought out Dutch consultants, because as Charles J. McGillycuddy wrote, "The entire country of Holland may be considered a clean steal from the sea.") In 1970, the *Hudson Dispatch* announced a plan for the Meadowlands with the headline CITY OF THE FUTURE, and William Cahill, then governor of New Jersey, predicted people would be so excited about living in the Meadowlands that there would be, in his words, "a mass exodus from New York." A pamphlet from about the same time was entitled *Turning Swamps into Dollars*. Most actual development of the meadows came in bits and pieces, though beginning in 1914 one large-scale development scheme converted most of Newark's meadows into modern Meadowlands. The city of Newark built dikes and used huge pipes to bury the gentle marsh grass in sand. I think of the old meadows now whenever I rent a car at Newark International Airport. As best I can tell, the rental car area is in the vicinity of a stream that once ran through the area. The stream was called Dead Creek.

One of the first people to attempt a large-scale development of the Meadowlands was Samuel N. Pike, a New York City real estate developer and distiller, who in 1866 founded the Iron Dike & Land Reclamation Company. Pike based his plans for the Meadowlands on a method of diking developed by Spencer B. Driggs, an inventor who was previously known for a piano that was supposed to sound like a violin. The centerpiece of Driggs's dikes were large iron plates. Previous large-scale attempts to dike the meadows had failed primarily because dikes made of soil or clay eroded or were chewed through by sand crabs and muskrats. Driggs's new method was cutting edge. "[I]t was left to an American to solve a problem which the genius and science of the Old World have labored at for hundreds of years in vain," one commentator said. Pike set about diking three thousand acres at a cost of a hundred dollars per acre, the manpower assembled to do so rivaling the feats of ancient Egyptians. "When properly drained, *the soil of these marshes will be the richest and most productive in the country,*" the company's prospectus predicted. In 1871, *The New York Times* reported the project was "progressing favorably, the tide water having been effectively shut out, a large tract of land plowed and some portion of it cropped, and the enterprise of bringing it into cultivation bids fair to be a success." But the great farmland never materialized. Instead of selling the reclamated land to farmers, Pike was forced to sell it to railroads, and then only at a loss. Pike's project is best remembered for the fact that while cornstalks grew well on his reclaimed land, the stalks produced not one ear of corn. A report on the state of the Meadowlands written in 1957 suggested that the iron dikes had disappeared by 1900. But in fact the swamp didn't destroy them; it made them its own. If you go out on the Hackensack River in a canoe at low tide and look around on the Kearny side of the river just north of the

New Jersey Turnpike bridge, you can spot them. They are bright, rusty red.

The patron saint of Meadowlands reclamators was General Robert Swartwout, who invested in the Meadowlands with his two brothers, Samuel and John. The Swartwouts were New York City scions at the time. Robert was friendly with Andrew Jackson, James Monroe, and Henry Clay, and he had been Quartermaster of the Army during the War of 1812. John, also a general, ran a paint business. Samuel was closely associated with Aaron Burr, having served as his secretary for a time, and he knew Andrew Jackson well enough to be appointed Collector of the Port of New York—a job that ended for him when he ran away to Europe in 1838, accused of swindling a million dollars to use in wild land speculation deals in Texas. The Swartwouts took sides in the political battles of the day by partaking in duels. John, for instance, dueled with DeWitt Clinton, who was a U.S. senator at the time, and ended up taking one of Clinton's bullets in his leg. Robert was more fortunate in his duel with Richard Riker, a onetime losing New York City mayoral candidate. The two squared off at the Weehawken dueling grounds where Alexander Hamilton dueled Aaron Burr, and Riker was the one who limped away—though perhaps not due to Robert's marksmanship. Riker reportedly shot himself in the foot.

The three brothers began buying small marshy plots in the Meadowlands with speculative purposes in mind, but by 1816 they had chartered a company called the Hackensack and Passaic Meadow Company to develop a system of drains and dikes. By 1819, they had built 7.5 miles of embankments, 120 miles of ditches, and enclosed two thousand acres, thirteen hundred of which were completely drained and ready for farming. The *New York Post* reported: "Grains of various kinds,

English grasses, garden vegetables and hemp and flax are found to grow in luxuriance, and no soil is better calculated for grazing." A letter to the *American Farmer*, an agricultural journal of the time, called it "one of the most magnificent undertakings that has ever distinguished the liberal spirit of this great state." Cows grazed on the Swartwouts' reclaimed land, and it was their intention to make the Meadowlands into a giant dairy farm for New York City—though when they turned to New York for financial help, the city turned them down. It was all downhill for the Swartwouts from there. Soon, an unusually high tide damaged the dikes and dike-eating muskrats began to infiltrate. The Swartwouts made an unsuccessful fund-raising trip to Holland and then began to grow impatient with one another. Samuel tried to sell his share, but Robert and John stopped him. In 1823, John died, his entire fortune, two hundred thousand dollars, sunk in the Meadowlands. When Samuel finally sold his share, only Robert was left. Robert became obsessed with the Meadowlands. "In a word," he wrote in a memo to himself, "these lands are too valuable to remain unimproved—they lie too near this splendid city to be abandoned—they must and shall be placed in a position to produce revenue. . . . I will nail my colors to the mast and conquer or perish with them."

Robert began to perish with the meadows after 1830. He had lost what remained of the Swartwouts original land to creditors and was borrowing money from Samuel to lease it back. In 1833, he founded the New York & Bergen Dairy Company, again with the goal of supplying New York City with "pure and wholesome milk." He continued writing memos. "Immense herds of cattle will be fatted for market," he wrote to himself on Sunday night in February 1833. He asked rhetorically shortly thereafter, "How can the success of such a work be denied when the most invincible proofs are before us?" As the New York & Bergen Dairy Company's lands were all now almost underwater, that company failed too, and so Swartwout next considered creating an animal husbandry school in the Meadowlands, the idea being that people on their way West from New York to settle the frontier would stop first on Swartwout's land to learn from him the art of farming. Samuel, who was just about to flee to Europe, wrote to Robert to say he was getting fed up. "You only waste time and means for nothing," Samuel said. Robert, who was married and had two children, was feeling less than optimistic himself, given that the once wealthy family was on the verge of homelessness; he signed a letter written around this time, "Yours very dull and low spirited." But eventually he rallied, responding to Samuel: "I have long set my heart upon this project on public grounds as well as personal, and you are the last person from whom objections are expected. . . . The projects of reclaiming the marshland in the valley of the Hackensack I have long had uppermost at my heart, and [it is] one which until it is accomplished will continue to receive my undivided attention; no consideration, personal or prospective, can divert me from its prosecution, and I therefore beseech you as a brother professing kind feelings . . . not to cross my path in this great object of my life." When Samuel fled to Europe, Robert went bankrupt.

Somehow Robert managed to find another set of backers and he continued to write memos to himself—on the possibility of constructing a brewery in the Meadowlands, on the specifications of the animal husbandry school, about the possibility of silk cultivation, of growing peaches, strawberries, tomatoes, asparagus, cucumbers, pumpkins, and lemons. He wrote himself a note titled: "Milk Required on the West Side of the City," which listed an order of forty gallons of milk for Tammany Hall, and he wrote to ask a friend who was said to have knowledge of Holland: "Does draining and sluicing hurt fish? What is best crop?" He began to think people were plotting to steal his land, which was still submerged. In all that he wrote, he continued to refer to his meadow-related ideas as "this great work." At some point, he seems to have realized that his personal life was suffering—his wife had died and his children were upset with him for squandering his money on his great work, and he was now living alone in cheap hotels. In yet another memo he wrote, "Having fully reflected on my solitary position in society, I am satisfied that the fault is my own and that if I wish to marry and seek as I ought to among the wealthy and the good I can soon find a companion and a wife, every way suitable to make my life an earthly paradise. Having come to this definitive conclusion, I will make it a duty no longer to be neglected, but to be followed out in the shortest reasonable time." He fulfilled his duty by writing the following letter, which he handed to various women in the street:

Dear Madam,

Need I say how ardently I love you? Have not my eyes, when they have met yours, long since proclaimed the secret? But how to get an interview to declare my passion has taxed my invention. I have finally concluded when I should meet you in the street unattended I would approach and speak and place in your hand this note . . .

Robert died of a stroke on July 17, 1848, still a widower. The government held on to his land for a few years vainly hoping to make a profit. Finally, what remained of Robert's claims was handed over to Hudson County. The county eventually built a poor farm on the land and then an insane asylum. A guidebook of the area published in 1896 said this about the Swartwouts' portion of the meadows: "These marshes were the scene of an experiment in farming which ruined a prosperous family many years ago." The entry quoted an old Secaucus resident as saying, "When in summer the train dashed across the miles of swamp land beyond Hoboken, and the long salt grass, jeweled with flowers of brilliant hue, sways and tosses to the breath of the wind, it seems to me, as I look out from the car window, as if the wild roses and the meadow grasses were growing over the graves of those buried hopes."

Gone with the Wind

I LIKE TO THINK OF THE MEADOWLANDS AS AN UNDESIGNATED national park, where you can visit all the sites, or as a more classic tourist destination, like Paris, where instead of roaming through old streets and wandering aimlessly through cafés and shops I wander along the edges of the swamps. One spring, I flew to Newark, rented a car, and checked into a hotel with the idea of touring around and just seeing where events would lead me. Like the Grand Canyon, with its North Rim and South Rim and their respective concentrations of lodgings, the Meadowlands pools its motels into two areas. Along the eastern edge of the Meadowlands are the seedy motels that cater mostly to truck drivers. These motels look out at the huge, flat center of the Meadowlands as if they have all just woken up and are still tired and really need a cup of coffee and a shower. Along the western edge, the hotels and motels stand tall and crisp and glass-covered; these are the business person—oriented hotels. To these hotels and motels the landscape is incidental, if not insignificant; they try to pretend the Meadowlands are not there.

The Days Inn in East Rutherford doesn't say so in its promotional literature, but it is located on the banks of Berry's Creek, a long, dark, and polluted creek that cuts through the particularly thick swamp grass behind the Meadowlands Sports Complex. I chose this particular hotel because it was reasonably priced and because it had recently undergone a typical Meadowlands experience. One night, the seventeen thousand gas canisters stored on the property next door to the Days Inn began blowing up. Shrapnel flew through the air. When asked to describe the sound of the explosions, a witness said it reminded him of hand grenades going off. Illustrating a central tenet of life in the Meadowlands—that not even the people who live and work there know for sure what is there—the local police and fire departments and an emergency response team of the New Jersey Department of Environmental Protection recommended evacuating the area. At 3 A.M., guests began leaving the hotel. As the explosions continued, two wedding parties eventually came out from the hotel into the parking lots. The brides, their white dresses in their hands, boarded a bus that took them to a local school. In the end, no one was hurt. As I checked into the Days Inn, I asked the hospitality manager about the explosion and subsequent evacuation. "It wasn't such a big deal," she said. Then I asked for a room with a view. At first she said she had no rooms with a view. A second later she corrected herself and gave me a room on the fourth floor. As I rode the elevator, another hospitality manager who had overheard my inquiries about the exploding canisters told me that among the people in the two wedding parties it took a particularly long time to evacuate one of the two brides and grooms from their room because they hadn't noticed any explosions.

My room was exquisitely nondescript. Like the motel itself, a gigantic concrete cube that would have seemed awkward and out of place in a rural Vermont countryside, the room blossomed on the shore of the meadows. The ceiling was an off-white inverted ocean, the peaks of textured plaster like thousands of little waves. The pattern on the drab plastic wall covering, also off-white, was a series of monotonously parallel indentations, like rows of gravel raked on a highway roadbed prior to paving. The window was located in the far corner, a structural afterthought, and through it I mostly saw a huge gray sky and thousands of acres of swamp. To the right was the yard of explosive canisters, the surviving canisters huddled in groups. To the east was Berry's Creek. When I went back down to the lobby and looked out the front window of the hotel, I could see a go-go bar through the small patch of swamp grass guarding the Days Inn. In fact, most of what I saw out most of the windows was a sea of reeds. This was my base camp.

I was soon making forays out into my view, and one of my first stops was to a field adjacent to the parking lot of the hotel, which was cordoned off with an orange plastic fence. Men wearing white plastic suits, bright yellow boots, and some kind of respirator or breathing device rummaged through this field. In my room, while drinking glass after glass of odd-tasting ice water, I had watched these men: they appeared to be walking in slightly slow motion, as if they were weightless, as if the land behind the orange fence were land on another world. After a while, I grabbed my key card, caught an elevator, and went outside to ask them what they were doing. When I approached the fence and attempted to

attract their attention, they all looked over at me, and one of
the men dropped a kind of rake and ran to me waving his
arms. "Don't come over here!" he shouted. I tried to explain
myself. He shouted louder this time: *"Don't come over here!"* He
was still waving his arms. I stood perfectly still, trying not to
make any moves that would alarm him.

When he arrived at my side, I explained that I was exploring the area and asked him what he was doing in the field.
"Nothing, really," he said. I asked him what was in the field
that was being dug up. He said, "Oh, just some old tires."
Then I asked him why, if there were just some old tires, he was
wearing a white plastic suit and bright yellow boots and all.

"Uhm," he said. He seemed to hesitate. "It's for the bugs.
You know, like ticks and stuff." He was nodding now. "It's just
a lot easier to see them crawling on you with these on."

"Uh huh," I said.

After that, I drove west down a road bordered by factories and
warehouses and ten-foot-tall reeds and only once saw a human:
a speed-walking woman with kinky, orangeish hair and a deep
salon tan who was wearing wraparound mirrored sunglasses and
neon-colored Nikes and a bright pink suit that stood out like the
plumage of a tropical songbird as it swished past the mono-
chromatic reeds. A big piece of plastic blew across the road like
a tumbleweed. Eventually, the road dead-ended in the swamp.
I got out of my car and walked into the tall grass, pressing it
behind me with great effort, and arrived at a couch that was purple and looked new and turned out to be very comfortable.

If you wander around in the Meadowlands for any amount of
time, if you move from one unattractive attraction to the
next, then you soon realize that outside of the swamp grass,
the sky is the most predominant feature of the Meadowlands.

The area's undevelopability has kept it relatively free of sky-scrapers and tall buildings. All over the Meadowlands, there is uninterrupted panorama. It's Big Sky Country East.

Giant AM radio antennae thrive in the open airspace that the Meadowlands offers—a race of lanky giants caught stealing across the swamp—because salt water readily conducts radio signals, and the salt marshes of the Meadowlands are the next best thing to salt water. Most of New York City's AM radio stations have their transmitters planted in the Meadowlands. One day, while meandering along the edge of an area in the Meadows known as the Kingsland Marsh, I knocked on the door of the rectangular-shaped control room of the broadcasting facility for WINS, a New York news radio station. I had watched over the course of a year as they replaced old antennae with new ones. The four new antennae were each four hundred feet tall, and buried in the marsh beneath each one were radial antennae, each of those jutting from the base of the tower every three degrees like the spokes of a submerged bicycle wheel. In the control room, I talked to Ken Bieber, a radio engineer who has worked on many of the new and old radio antennae in the Meadowlands. He was chewing a sandwich beneath a walrusy mustache; he had a dry sense of humor, which he exhibited when I mentioned to him that I thought the new antennae looked great.

"You must not be with the housing authority," he said.

He said this because these particular giant antennae were controversial. Most giant radio antennae in the Meadowlands are painted red and white so that low-flying airplanes don't hit them, but the residents of the development on the ridge facing these towers, called Meadow Ridge, thought a giant red-and-white antenna would ruin their view of the meadows, and they asked that the towers be painted a color that would match the color of the Meadowlands sky. The towers were painted gray. Then, a few weeks later, local authorities determined that the gray towers blended in *too* well with the sky and were a hazard to planes. Now Meadow Ridge residents stare out at the only radio towers in the Meadowlands with lights that blink day and night.

Sometimes when I'm out in the Meadowlands, I feel as if I'm in a *National Geographic* special and I'm visiting little tribes of people unknown to everyone else, the traditions of whom are unfamiliar to me. I met one tribelike group as I was driving along a factory-bordered road in Moonachie (pronounced *moon-ah-kee*). I was on my way to Little Ferry to watch the sun set on the ponds that fill the old clay pits and was driving through an area that used to be covered with farms and owned mostly by Captain John Berry, a British emigrant from Barbados who was a captain in the Newark Militia and amassed so many acres of meadows that he gave a chunk of it away as a wedding gift. I was lost when I discovered a little field with a wind sock next to a place called Losen Slote, Dutch for winding creek. Losen Slote winds through one of the least developed portions of the meadows, a tiny biosphere for old Meadowlands flora and fauna. To naturalists, this area is known for wildflowers such as the sweet-rooted marshmallow. To model airplane pilots, Losen Slote is the water hazard near the main runway of the Hackensack Valley Model Aerodrome.

A local mechanic flew a sleek, low-flying racing craft, its Day-Glo orange streamers teasing the flaglike phragmites flower on the afternoon I visited the aerodrome. Another pilot was a sculptor whose studio is in the Chelsea section of Manhattan. He was flying a Piper Cub–like plane that he had bought wounded at a garage sale in the Hamptons, on Long Island, and had nursed back to health. You could tell the plane had spent time flying over a beach because it had little make-believe advertisements painted on its wings. The sculptor told me he keeps in touch with the control tower at Teterboro Airport as he works in his studio during the day, and when the weather is right he heads out through the Lincoln Tunnel and is taxiing up his plane in thirty-five minutes. On this day, the wings of his plane shuttered as it took off into a stiff wind.

I was enjoying watching the model planes take off over the Losen Slote, and the other planes high in the sky and the sunset and the futuristic-looking skyline of New York until another pilot grabbed me away. He pointed across the meadows to an old railway tunnel that I couldn't see and told me that he had once walked it in its entirety, entering in the Meadowlands and using a flashlight in the damp dark to guide him all the way to the shore of the Hudson River. For protection, he said, he carried a gun.

One night in my hotel I wrote a postcard to a friend and told him about how, what with all the chemicals and gas lines and refineries out in the Meadowlands, I was always wondering if I was going to see something explode. A short time later, on another trip to Moonachie, I almost did. I was making my way down a street of warehouses toward a swamp, when I was stopped by a policeman, whose car was parked at an angle with its lights spinning in order to block people from proceeding. I asked him if I could pass. He shook his head, pointed behind him, and said very matter-of-factly, "There's a possibility that this building might blow up." Not long after that, when I was near Harrison one day on the edge of the Kearny Marsh, I passed a company called S.O.S. Gases. In front of S.O.S. Gases, the tanks stand like rocket ships, poised for takeoff. On that day, they were all of a sudden surrounded by white gas that made the parking lot look like the dry-iced floor of an old disco. When I rolled my window down, I heard the tanks say, *Shhhhhhh!*

Notes from a train ride across the Meadowlands just after a big snowstorm one winter that covered the Meadowlands with whiteness, when I sat behind a man who was giving the people he was sitting with a tour of the view: The man described the tanks and the giant coal piles, which rise and fall seasonally depending on home heating needs. He spoke with great authority. We were crossing the Hackensack River when he said to his friends, "You know, when there's snow out there, this place almost looks human."

A MEADOWLANDS DRAMA,
overheard after driving around for a long time and pulling into a diner on the edge of the swamp for coffee.

CHARACTERS: A husband and wife and their waitress as they discuss Amish settlements in Pennsylvania. (The waitress, who was Vietnamese, had never heard of the Amish before.)

WIFE: They will shun you. If you don't follow their rules they will shun you.
WAITRESS: They kill?
WIFE: No, they don't kill. They shun.
WAITRESS: How far away is it?
WIFE: About three hours.
HUSBAND: *(With mouth full.)* Beautiful country.
WAITRESS: Anywhere except for here is beautiful.

Kearny is one of my favorite towns in the Meadowlands. I could wander around Kearny for days. Kearny is three-quarters

Meadowlands, one-quarter town. The quarter that is town is a lot nicer than people who know nothing of the Meadowlands would believe. Many of the houses up the hill from the meadows are clean and neat and charming in a small-town kind of way. Inside the main branch of the Kearny post office, there is a mural that features a man working at a machine, his muscles flexed as he reaps the harvest of industry that is fed by the panoramic backdrop of Meadowlands. I just liked to poke around aimlessly in Kearny until the day when I read in an old guidebook that the Kearny Library was home to the world's largest collection of foreign translations of *Gone with the Wind*. Everything changed when I read that; all of a sudden I had a purpose in Kearny. I immediately drove across town to the Kearny Library, but the *Gone with the Wind* collection was nowhere to be found. Displayed in the little main hallway was instead an exhibit of photographs from the Kearny High School that featured a photo of a couple embracing on the Kearny Marsh; it was entitled "Love in the Meadows," and as I stared at it realized it was set on an abandoned dump. At the front desk, no one had the slightest idea where the world's largest collection of foreign translations of *Gone with the Wind* was. But they said they'd find out.

I waited in the local history section of the Kearny Library, where I passed the time reading about the town's namesake, General Philip Kearny, the great one-armed general, who resided for many years in Kearny in Bellegrove, a château modeled after a home he had seen in France. Kearny was one of those guys who isn't happy unless he's fighting in a war somewhere. This was evident early on in Kearny's case, when he attended a private school opposite West Point and spent his spare time gazing longingly across the river at the cadets. His grandfather wanted him to be a minister. They struck a compromise, and Kearny studied to be a lawyer, albeit a lawyer who enjoyed riding horses at death-defying speeds while pretending he was in a war somewhere. Still, when he finished school and traveled through Europe with his cousin, Kearny only wanted to go to the military parades. When his grandfather died and left him a millionaire, Kearny immediately enlisted in the army. In 1839, the secretary of war sent Kearny to France to study tactics. There he learned to ride with his reins in his teeth so that he could wield his sword in one hand and his pistol in the other. In France, he became known as Kearny *le Magnifique*.

In 1841, Kearny married Diana Bullitt, and they had four children in forty-eight months. Bullitt insisted Kearny resign from the army. Kearny refused initially, then resigned—but only for a few weeks, because in 1846 the United States went to war with Mexico and he had another reason to enlist. Kearny went to work rounding up some horses with a young lawyer he knew in Illinois named Abraham Lincoln, and he started a cavalry troop that soon became known as the finest in the United States—Company F, 1st U.S. Dragoons. One night during the war, Kearny joked that he'd give his left arm for a chance to charge at the enemy. The next day his unit was ordered to storm the gates of Mexico City. The order was rescinded but Kearny either didn't hear or ignored it. As he charged, he was hit in the left arm, a single ball of shot shattering the bone between his elbow and his shoulder. The next day, General Franklin Pierce held his head while Kearny's arm was amputated. He returned to New York, where he worked as a recruiting officer, which he didn't enjoy. His marriage began to disintegrate. Then, against his wife's wishes, he took an assignment fighting the Rogue River Indians in Oregon. After that, he began wandering the globe from conflict to conflict. Back in France, he went to a ball in Paris in the Tuileries and met Agnes Maxwell, the daughter of Hugh Maxwell, who was then the customs director for the Port of New York. It is said that when they met, Agnes was so taken by the appearance of Kearny, decked out in military regalia, his regal chin jutting out in his trademark *le Magnifique* style, that she fainted, and Kearny reached out and caught her with his good arm.

Maxwell was twenty years old at the time, so their relationship inspired much gossip in the New York papers. Kearny attempted to divorce Bullitt, but she refused. Kearny was so depressed about the matter that he went into seclusion on family property in upstate New York, where, while riding, he fell through a bridge and nearly killed himself. Agnes rushed to his side to nurse him back to health. They moved in together, at Bellegrove, on the ridge in Kearny that overlooks the Passaic on its way into the Meadowlands. Agnes became pregnant, which caused a huge scandal. In 1855, they left for Europe in separate carriages. (Bullitt finally agreed to divorce Kearny in 1858, and Kearny and Maxwell were married in Paris.) In 1859, France aided Italy in its war against Austria, and Kearny jumped at the chance to enlist and ride again toward enemy lines. "I participated in every charge that took place," he proudly wrote in a letter. He and Agnes returned to America when the Civil War broke out, and Kearny was given charge of the New Jersey regiment; George Custer was his aide-de-camp. Kearny family legend has it that his son, John Watts Kearny, hated his father so much for exposing his mother to public ridicule by living with Agnes that he attempted to join the Confederate Army so he would have a chance to shoot his father. (Kearny scholars refute this by pointing out that the younger Kearny was at school in Europe at the time.) Some historians like to speculate that Kearny might have been assigned to lead the Union forces instead of Ulysses S. Grant, given Kearny's friendship with Lincoln, had he not continued his practice of charging enemy lines, which was becoming even more extravagant. On one occasion, he charged out and rode up and down the front with his sword in the air as the enemy's shot missed him and killed two of his aides. Finally, his luck gave out. He charged a Confederate line and discovered that he was lost. He asked the nearest soldiers which side they were on. The soldiers were Confederate soldiers, and they told him they were on the Confederate side and suggested he not run. "You are crazy, man," one of the Confederate soldiers reportedly said. "You can't get ten feet."

"Sir, I have a good horse here and can depend on him every time. He'll carry me through," Kearny replied.

With that, Kearny turned and rode. The Confederate soldiers shot him. Kearny hadn't gotten ten feet.

When he arrived at the scene, A. P. Hill, a Confederate general, gave the two Confederate soldiers what sounds like a reprimand. "My God, boys," he said. "You know whom you have killed? You shot the most gallant officer in the United States Army. This is Phil Kearny." After he said this, General Hill took off his hat, as did everyone else who was present.

The librarians working the front desk came back with the head librarian, who had heard of the world's largest collection of foreign translations of *Gone with the Wind* but didn't know exactly where it was. The collection had recently been packed away by the library's custodian, and he was out of the building on an errand. I had no choice but to wait some more, during which time I pondered the town of Kearny's world-renowned reputation for soccer, the subject of another exhibition in the

Kearny Library that day. In some ways, Kearny is as much a municipality in the Meadowlands as it is a farm team for world-class soccer players. More soccer players have come out of Kearny than anywhere else in America. In an effort to kill time, I asked the librarian if there was anyone in town I could talk to about Kearny and soccer, and she sent me down to the Scottish-American Club where her husband was tending bar that afternoon.

During subsequent trips to Kearny, I would learn a lot about its soccer legacy. I would learn, for instance, that soccer was first played in Kearny in the early 1900s when a number of Scots came to work at an old thread mill and started up a soccer league with other factories. Kearny men were on the U.S. Olympic soccer team as long ago as 1924, and in 1992 three people from Kearny made the U.S. Olympic soccer team—John Harkes, Tab Ramos, and Tony Meola, and Harkes and Ramos were on again in 1996. Harkes went on to be a professional player, as did many other Kearny soccer stars, and almost everyone in town claims to have coached Harkes at one time or another. In fact, he is even a kind of sex symbol in Kearny, if only because all the men in Kearny think all the women in Kearny consider him to be such. After Meola played in the Olympics, he went to New York to become an actor but then got back into soccer because the acting career didn't pan out—Kearnyites roll their eyes when they tell Meola's story. Once, in a plastics factory on the Kearny Marsh, I talked with Hugh O'Neal, whom I only later learned is one of Kearny's greatest players and once played against Pelé. Another time, I was driving along the edge of the swamp late one night and spotted a white glow emanating from a field in Kearny. There, I came upon a team of Kearny residents in their mid- to late thirties playing a team from

Garfield, New Jersey, while a bunch of old Scottish guys on the sidelines laughed and cheered. Turf exploded off the field; grunts echoed in the moist Meadowlands air. A Kearny breakaway! Shoot! *Score!*

But at the Scottish-American Club that the librarian kindly directed me to that day, when I asked about the history of Kearny soccer and was pointed toward a Scottish gentlemen who was sitting on a stool at the bar with a half-gone pint of ale and who promptly and amiably discussed the secret of Kearny's soccer success with me, I am sorry to say that I didn't learn a whole lot about Kearny and soccer. This was simply because I don't speak either Scottish or drunk Scottish. During our chat, I picked out the words *television* and *Kearny* and *soccer.* He punctuated his remarks with the phrase "Thaws *sheet!*"

"Thaws *sheet!*" he said.

"I'm sorry?" I said, begging his pardon and indicating that I hoped he would repeat himself.

"Thaws *sheet!*" he said again.

I nodded and ordered up a beer.

When the library's custodian returned and took me down into the basement and showed me several dusty boxes filled with books, I dove in. For a while, a couple of librarians watched me, but then they left and I was alone with the world's largest collection of foreign translations of *Gone with the Wind.*

The first thing you notice about the Kearny Library's *Gone with the Wind* collection is that each edition seems like a completely different book, judging by the covers. The Japanese editions stand out if only for their diversity and their sharp, colorful covers. The first one I picked up featured a painting by Monet, which made me think I might be reading a wonderful Civil War—less novel about a romantic afternoon somewhere in France. Yet another had a painting by van Gogh. My favorite Japanese translation seemed less like a steamy Southern drama than a home decorating book. Inside, on the cover page, was a picture of an impeccably dressed Japanese woman seated in a comfortable chair adjacent to a table topped with orchids in a vase; according to a translator I spoke with a few days ago, the caption beneath her read, "The author enjoys the English edition of the book"—even though the woman seemed a little too Japanese to be the Southern author. Likewise, the introduction to the Chinese edition described Margaret Mitchell as "modest, pure, and benevolent" and as a perfect housekeeper. The Italian edition looked like something a seedy businessman might purchase in an airport bookstore and carry on to the plane in a brown paper bag; it featured a sultry portrait of Vivian Leigh, her lips pursed, her eyebrow arched. (If you don't know Italian, the text sounds pretty sultry too, especially when read aloud alone in the basement of the Kearny Library: *"Rosella O'Hara non era una bellezza;"* the book began, *"ma raramente gli uomini se ne accorgevano . . ."*) Meanwhile, the texts seemed drastically different in meaning, even to a nonlinguist. Vietnam's Cuốn Theo Chiều Gió had a first sentence that was Proustian in length—"Scarlett O'HARA *không có duroc một vẻ dẹp cô-diên, nhurng, dàn ông ho không nhân ra chỗ ây, khi mà, cũng nhur hai anh em sanh dôi nhà* TARLETON, *ho da bi duyên-dáng của nàng thu-phuc"*—while the Latvian translator was with his first sentence more Hemingwayesque: *"Skarletu Ohāru īstenī ba nevarēja saukt par skaistuli."*

I discovered later that the foreign translations of *Gone with the Wind* became both the bane and the delight of Margaret Mitchell's writing career. "It never occurred to me that *Gone with the Wind* would be translated into any foreign language," she wrote in a letter. "When it appeared in so many languages and had such astoundingly good reviews, I was breathless, and still am." She had every reason to be breathless, given that people all over the world wanted to read her novel. The French reportedly read more copies of *Gone with the Wind* than any other book during the German occupation, and, in 1944, in Norway, Holland, Belgium, and France, the book sold for as much as sixty dollars on the black market. The Germans, who bought many copies of it themselves, were ordered to confiscate the book, and some people were shot for *Gone with the Wind* possession. After the war, Mitchell wrote, "The *Gone with the Wind*" rights in Europe have turned out to be more valuable, potentially, since the war than before, for every country has had its recent experience with war and occupations and defeat, and people in each country apply the experiences of the characters of *Gone with the Wind* to themselves." Unfortunately, tracking down all the foreign publishers and attempting to stop pirating apparently wore her down. In 1947, she wrote, "I can feel it in the wind when foreign publishers are getting ready to bring out unauthorized editions of *Gone with the Wind.*" In a letter she wrote toward the end of her life, she complained that sorting out all the foreign rights had been one of the reasons she never published another novel. She died in 1949, after being hit by a car.

I closed up all the *Gone with the Wind*s and went back upstairs exuberant. Now a librarian came forth with the story of the origin of the collection. Harold Latham had discovered Margaret Mitchell and published her at Macmillan, where he was an editor, and Latham lived and died in Kearny. Mitchell, the librarian had told me, always sent copies of the foreign translations to Latham and he eventually donated them to his local library, where they faded away. I said good-bye to several librarians triumphantly and they wished me luck on my trips through the Meadowlands as they simultaneously checked out big piles of books and videotapes to teenagers. As I was walking out the door, one librarian said to another, "I didn't know we had those, did you? Maybe we should bring them upstairs."

Walden Swamp

IN THE MIDDLE OF THE MEADOWLANDS, THERE IS A PLACE called Walden Swamp. For a long time, I only stared at it on my map. I asked about Walden Swamp in libraries and at city halls, but people in the area who knew that section of the Meadowlands either had never heard of it referred to by any name or they didn't really care. It's difficult to care about Walden Swamp in that there are no roads into Walden Swamp, and it is impossible to hike there. To get to Walden Swamp you pretty much have to take some kind of a boat, which was what I started to think I ought to do. I began to consider taking a trip to Walden Swamp and then spending some time out there and maybe even contemplating nature and civilization just like Thoreau, or someone like that. With my maps, with similar questions about the other seemingly unexplored areas that surrounded it, I began to think of the Meadowlands as a completely unexplored place. Pretty soon I was calling up my friend Dave, who is tall and athletic and up for almost anything when it comes to an adventure in an industrial swamp, and we were planning expeditions into Walden Swamp, into the heart of the Meadowlands.

We planned two expeditions: one to Walden Swamp, up in the northern reaches of the unroaded swamp, and another from Snake Hill in Secaucus to the baseball diamond in Kearny. We did the second trip first because it seemed more ambitious. It was a trip across the waist of the Meadowlands, if you think of the Meadowlands as someone who's built like a barrel and has short legs. I had read accounts of people taking trips across the Meadowlands, but usually the accounts were by early settlers who did so in little sailboats. As far as I knew, no one had ever attempted to cross the Meadowlands since the highways and dikes and the New Jersey Turnpike had been built—at least there were no records that I could find of such crossings in the modern era.

If Lewis and Clark were planning an expedition across the Meadowlands, they would have had a head start because presumably they would already have had access to a canoe. I had initially hoped to rent one for a few days, but I encountered some resistance to this idea in the local boat rental community: I called up a boat rental place in Hackensack, New Jersey, and told them I wanted to rent a boat to use in the Meadowlands, and the woman answering the phone said, "What are you, *crazy?*" So I ended up driving up the Hackensack River Valley one day to Campmor, a giant outdoor activity supply store, in Paramus, where I intended to buy just a canoe, so as not to interfere with my Meadowlands experiment—Thoreau's exhortation to simplify was nagging at me—but where I ended up buying a lot of other stuff—I mean, as long as I was there:

1 Silva precision compass $9.99

1 Deet Plus™ PROFESSIONAL Insect Repellent $3.29

Seal Line Dry Bag (smoke-tinted) $9.99

4 PowerBars® "Athletic Energy Food, Fuel for Optimum

    Performance" @ $1.00 each $4.00

1 Tillamook peppered beefsteak jerky $1.50

1 Pur® Scout™ Antimicrobial water purifier $79.00

1 SweetWater Silt-Stopper $9.99

1 Fisher Space Pen, "as used on all manned space flights:

    American and Russian" $5.99

1 All-weather Shirt Pocket Spiral Memo Pad $2.50

1 Mad River canoe $450.00

2 Stearns Personal Flotation Devices $13.99

2 oars @ $12.50 . . . .$25.00

Total price of a canoeing expedition in the Meadowlands: $615.24

While at Campmor, I had a difficult time choosing a water purification system. A middle-aged bearded man who was not an employee of Campmor and who was dressed as if he were in the middle of a summer camping trip through the Rockies kept offering me advice and I kept telling him he didn't understand my water purification needs. Undaunted, he pulled one device off a shelf, held it in my face, and said, "Well, this one can handle anything. I used it once in the mountains in Idaho and there was a *lot* of animal scat around there." He wouldn't stop bugging me, so finally I blurted out that I was going on a trip through the Meadowlands. At that, he moved away from me slowly, toward the camping stove section.

When I asked a Campmor salesperson if a particular water filter would allow me to drink the water in the Meadowlands, he said, "It should," and nonchalantly shrugged his shoulders. I felt that he didn't understand the water purification stakes I was about to face, so I asked to speak to his supervisor, who was then summoned by storewide intercom. I waited while the salesperson acted annoyed. The supervisor recommended combining two purification devices together, saying he had seen this technique used once by someone who drank water from a pond in Central Park in New York. That sounded a little haphazard to me, so to clarify the matter, I asked him if such a filter would protect me from poisoning myself in the Meadowlands. "Yes," he said, and then added, "I mean, it should."

In the canoe department, I picked out a big red polyethylene canoe.

I strapped the canoe to my rental car and started out early on the morning of our first adventure. I picked up Dave, who had taken a train to New Jersey from Brooklyn, where he lives, and together we loaded the canoe with supplies and dropped it in the Hackensack River just below Snake Hill. Having never canoed in the Hackensack before, we were a little surprised that the canoe even floated; Dave imagined that the water would somehow eat away the bottom of the canoe, that it would dissolve the oars like acid. Nothing like that happened, though. We pushed off from the shore of reeds and into the river. I was in front, Dave was in back (aside from being related to Meriwether Lewis, he earned the Boy Scout merit badge for canoeing). It was a cool summer day, with low formless clouds the color of steam. We felt like intruders, as if we had broken into an industrial landscape where bright colors weren't allowed. The strip of the eight-lane New Jersey Turnpike, a great arc across the long horizon, ruled like a mysterious god. From above, on the turnpike bridge, a couple of people waiting next to their broken-down van shouted down at us through the white noise of the traffic: "Canoe! Canoe!" And then an invisible police loudspeaker shouted back at them: *"Stay with your car! Please! Stay with your car!"*

The water was chocolate milk brown; I saw bits of wood and Styrofoam, two juice bottles, and clump after clump of broken reeds. Apropos of all the garbage and broken reeds in the river, Dave asked, "Which is flotsam and which is jetsam?" and I couldn't say. The current was quiet but ferocious; it swirled around our oars as we fought against it to cross under a railroad bridge with a charred-steak black frame. Once through, we signaled to the bridge operator, who had been watching us from his lonely, house-shaped booth, and asked him if the body of water behind him was the Kearny Marsh. "It's a marsh, and it's in Kearny," he said. "That's all I know." He then showed us the little cove in the river that he and his bridge-tending partner use to nurse ducks who come to him wounded by shotgun blasts. "We spoil them," he said, as we paddled by. The bridge tender would be the only human we would encounter traveling across the marsh that day.

Just past the train bridge, we portaged for the first time. We lugged the canoe up out of the river, up a bank, and across a nameless little road not marked on the maps. From there, we could see the whole panorama of this portion of the Meadowlands: a low, flat series of lakes bounded by train tracks and roads and fringed with tall reeds. There were radio towers ahead of us and high-tension lines picking up speed as they raced across the skyscraperless sky. Far off, the ridges were dotted with the houses in the little towns—onetime shorefront property on prehistoric Lake Hackensack. We stood for a while beneath the tall cement legs of the turnpike. Distant airhorns blasted, set off by train track workers nowhere to be seen, and the sound seemed like the sad calls of undiscovered birds.

When you are on the turnpike as it crosses over the Meadowlands, it can feel like the most frantic place in the world. But
there beneath the road, from where we stood astride our canoe,
the turnpike's work seemed calm and methodical and Zen.

We soon calculated that we were still far from the Kearny
Marsh and that we had several unnamed bodies of water to cross
yet, and while considering our next move we were startled by
a tide gate underneath the little road that suddenly belched river
water out into this first unnamed marsh. When we put into the
water, we found it without current, less brown and more dark
gray. And, because it was located under the Atlantic flyway for
automobiles, it functioned as a giant outdoor ashtray: the
waterlogged cigarette butts were bloated and curled as if
impersonating shrimp. I saw a three-inch-thick rusted cable
sticking up out of the water like a water snake. I also saw a golf
ball, the word FLOATER printed on it. Dave spotted an egret, its
long curved white neck the shape of a highway off-ramp, its
white feathers the color of Styrofoam. When the egret saw us,
it took off to the southwest, toward the smokestacks we could
just see in the faraway distance that was Newark.

The very idea of being in a canoe in the waters off the New
Jersey Turnpike was viscerally thrilling, but this thrill was
counterbalanced by a gnawing consideration of the toxicity of
the environment, the end result being a kind of nervous ten-
sion that gripped us as we paddled through the marshes. Dave
was the first to voice concern; he spoke after we inhaled a dank,
sewery smell that seemed to have been stirred up by our pad-
dles. "I feel like I just knocked a couple of years off my life,"
Dave said. But as we spotted more and more birds, we grew
more at ease, even if many of the birds seemed as anxious as we
were. We began to notice the tail ends of muskrats as they paddled for cover in their huts. In addition to the traffic sounds of

the turnpike, we soon heard splashing sounds, which we eventually determined to be spawning carp. Thrashing around in the foul-smelling muck, the carp, each approximately two feet long, did not seem at all out of place beneath the New Jersey Turnpike; the scales on their backs were gross and coarse in the pattern of worn-down radial tires. In about half an hour, when we came to the next impoundment, we tied up to a rusty I–beam that jutted from the bank of reeds, took our maps from the dry bag, and carefully considered the next leg of our trip.

We entered our second marsh, which was similar to the first, except perhaps more reed filled. I later learned that these small bodies of impounded water were formed at random, by the construction of railroad lines and the new and old turnpikes, but from the vantage point of our canoe at that moment, this seemed as natural a way to form a body of water as any. It was here, in the second swamp, that we came upon our first stumps from the Meadowlands old cedar forest. The stumps floated like corpses, their roots disappearing in the dark water. We poked at their tentacles with our oars, as a couple of red-winged blackbirds looked on suspiciously. A few minutes later, in a spot far from roads and highways, we discovered little islands, composed wholly of reeds. One island was surrounded by bright yellow police emergency tape: CAUTION, the tape said. Another island was inhabited by a lonely six-foot stepladder. In the next marsh, before an audience of terns, we canoed past the submerged control room of a radio transmission station, its giant antenna felled in the water like a child's broken toy. In the water below our canoe, we could just make out fences topped with barbed wire. I knew this to be the remains of one of the oldest radio antennae in the Meadowlands, thought to be the first to ever broadcast the voice of Frank Sinatra. When we approached Belleville Turnpike, we pulled our canoe and all our gear up over a four-foot-wide pipe that carried the water supply of Jersey City, and then, with the boat on our shoulders, we ran, timing our dash across the highway with the break in the waves of cars and trucks.

Using our compass and the power lines to guide us, we canoed more, portaged again, came to a patch of land marked as water on our maps, and then crossed an abandoned railroad track, at which time it was close to noon. We were beginning to think that we had arrived on the eastern edge of the Kearny Marsh, which meant that we had another mile to go in our trip; however, our maps were proving not terribly accurate with regard to navigable water routes. Around us there were green hills of grass-covered garbage dumps. We saw more carp, more muskrats, mudflats covered with sandpipers, and the frozen-in-time remains of a snapping turtle that appeared to have been decapitated by a train just as it had crawled up out of the marsh. We also saw a Thermos, three unopened cans of Pepsi, a beach chair sitting on another island, and a Seven Seas Red Wine Vinegar salad dressing spill. Passing over more underwater fences, we felt as if we were paddling just above Atlantis. At precisely one hour and fifty-two minutes into the trip, we saw our first abandoned appliance, a refrigerator. At one point, looking back on the Belleville Turnpike, its cars and trucks streaking by more starkly than those on the New Jersey Turnpike, which had now faded into the distance south of us, I saw a police car with its lights on and a long row of headlights led by a hearse. We felt alone and far away. And given that we were having trouble finding our place on our maps, we also felt lost.

*   *   *

The center of the Kearny Marsh was a maze of reeds, cut with channels to we didn't know where. Some of these channels were on the maps, some weren't, and taking any of them seemed to be a gamble. When we realized things weren't going well, we took a break and ate some PowerBars and were surprised by a FedEx jet as it lurched from out of a flock of low-flying clouds and let down its landing gear. We next put our faith in one long channel, which headed south. For a time, this seemed to work; the channel turned into a canal—we paddled long clean strokes and pushed ahead swiftly. But the big channel got small quickly and we were lost in the maze again. Twice, we got down on our knees in the canoe and grabbed stalks of phragmites and rocked and pulled and inched our way through bulbous mud-covered reed roots. We soon grew to despise the reeds, and the carps' thrashing began to sound sinister, as if they knew something we didn't.

The low point of the expedition came when we found ourselves in a shallow sewerlike creek, the bottom of which was completely covered with garbage. It was disgusting, to say the least. It was a hidden berm of trash, a refuse-strewn Sargasso Sea, and as we paddled, huge chunks of ripe debris rose up, as if from a field of underwater cabbages: a foul borscht. The smell was unbearable, and we paddled carefully. We pulled up onto an unmarked dirt road, and when we put in on the other side, we were relieved to find the water refreshingly murky again. In a few minutes, I could see a junkyard I thought might be in Kearny. Dave spotted ball field lights. I saw two boys fishing. I shouted out, "Hello there! What town are we in?" They said, "Kearny," and watched us curiously as we passed in our canoe. Finally, there was a break in the reeds and we landed. Four hours and one minute after leaving Secaucus, we stepped onto shore on the other side of the Meadowlands.

We ate lunch on a picnic bench with a view of a Kearny playground that was filled with children playing Little League baseball. When it came time to purify water from the marsh, we filled a container with the light greenish marsh liquid and watched particles of various shapes, sizes, and colors float through it. After we pumped this water through the filters, we looked at it for a long time, debating whether to drink it at all. Dave was the first to try the water. He just took a little sip and spit most of it out. I held it in a paper coffee cup in my hand for a long, long time and stared into it. When I finally poured the liquid into my mouth, I thought it tasted kind of funny, so I spit it out even faster than Dave. As seconds passed and I remained alive and felt no ill effects, I began to feel triumphant, as if something spiritual had happened, and I began praising the water filter and saying things like, "How bad could the water be, anyway?" I was still feeling that way about the water when a man came up to us as we were getting back into the boat and asked where we had come from. We pointed to Snake Hill far off in the distance. He told us that it was once a rite of passage for kids from Kearny to attempt to cross the meadows by walking all the way to Snake Hill on the railroad tracks. He also told us that there was a time when you could drop a rock in the Kearny Marsh and it would make a *splop* rather than a *splash* sound and that the marsh was known locally for many years as Shit Creek.

We began our trip back across the Meadowlands, putting in alongside an abandoned toilet fixture. We tried another route, which turned out to make the going easier in the Kearny Marsh but more difficult elsewhere: we ended up carrying the canoe for about a quarter of a mile alongside a long, steel railroad fence that looked abandoned and weary, as if it had been roughed up by the wind for decades. By dusk, we were back in the Hackensack River. We were all set to cross over to Snake Hill, to the point where our car was parked, until we came to the mouth of Saw Mill Creek, a tributary of the Hackensack at the entrance of an area known as the Kingsland Marsh. The mouth was decorated with gentle green strands of spartina, the last relatives of the Meadowlands' original meadow. The area was so starkly different from all that we had seen that day that we were leery of entering; we were shocked by its pristineness, by the absence of the tall, obnoxious reeds. When we finally moved into it, it was as if we had just come out of a trance. The water was shallow now, at low tide, the floor of the marsh a creamy gray, dotted with the borings of little creatures. A shiver ran down my spine. It all seemed strangely natural.

Our next expedition, to Walden Swamp, a short time later, took us into the northwestern quadrant of the Meadowlands on a small river called Berry's Creek. In contrast to our trip across the broad but impenetrable Kearny Marsh, this trip seemed to be along an easily followed route: Berry's Creek and its man-made tributary, Berry's Creek Canal, would lead us west, then north, then back onto another creek that led east to the Hackensack. Mercury is the key landscape ingredient in this area of the Meadowlands. Berry's Creek is sometimes called the Meadowlands' most polluted waterway. In the headwaters of Berry's Creek, in a town called Wood-Ridge, there was once a mercury dump and as recently as 1980, it was possible to dig a hole in the ground and watch it fill with balls of shiny silvery stuff. Approximately three hundred tons of mercury filtered down into the meadows by 1980, covering a total of forty acres of land and filling the livers and kidneys of Meadowlands' fish. At the old factory site where the mercury was actually dumped, humans suffered too—one worker lost the ability to speak, and a member of the crew hired to demolish the factory had to be hospitalized. Wood-Ridge residents were concerned that mercury might get into the basements of nearby homes during heavy rainstorms. News reports discussed the possibility of mercury evaporating, which in turn gave rise to questions about the effects of long-term exposure to the air in the Meadowlands. In 1979, many people in Wood-Ridge had samples taken of their urine and their hair. Today, the headwater of Berry's Creek is a land of Superfund cleanup sites and state remediation areas. State officials no longer consider the mercury to be a threat as long as it stays settled deep in the swamp's sediments. We hoped to canoe through this area, and, if possible, stop in Walden Swamp along the way. Energized from the success of our previous expedition across the Meadowlands, we looked over our maps confidently on the morning we set out, thinking maybe we could.

The day was hot and clear. We put in our canoe on the Hackensack River on the northern end of Secaucus between an apartment complex and a cement plant. While we were gearing up, a man in his late fifties parked his car next to us and tried to convince me to leave my car keys on top of my front tire. He assured me they would be perfectly safe there but I kept my keys in my pocket and watched the man mutter and pace back and forth on shore as we began paddling south—passing ducks, the backs of outlet stores, and a set of Hess oil tanks, both protected by floating yellow link-sausage-shaped oil spill containment devices. Once again there were roads all around us but the river was quiet. We passed beneath a highway interchange and lay on our backs admiring the sky as it was outlined by three elevated highways: I saw an arrowhead, Dave saw the pointer that you move around with a mouse on a computer screen. When we turned off the Hackensack and onto Berry's Creek Canal and began our trip into the north-west, we steered the canoe toward the banks and secretly observed the migratory patterns of the cars.

Soon we were in Walden Swamp, which was initially disappointing because it seemed to be just more monotonous corridors of reeds. The stagnant water was brown and marbleized with green and white and dotted with tapioca bead-like bits of wading Styrofoam. We passed a small school of giant plastic soda bottles. At around 11 A.M., we saw ahead of us the sole of a boot, floating ominously. On closer inspection, we could see that it was attached only to a desperate bit of algae, the first sign of nonreed, photosynthetic life we'd seen. When we reached the center of Walden Swamp, I was still determined to leave the boat and commune with nature and what have you. However, this turned out to be impossible because the shore wasn't a shore at all, but a giant mat of phragmites. We paddled through Walden Swamp slowly and quietly instead, looking down the canals that ran off its main tributary to catch a quick glimpse of some piece of the New York City skyline, which from Walden Swamp looked less like New York and more like Oz. At one point, midtown lined up with a view of an old Coca-Cola sign, and the coincidence seemed of astrological significance.

The Meadowlands Sports Complex loomed over the swamp. To be sure, Walden Swamp is not what it once was. It once was a cedar forest. Still, from our canoe, it seemed pristine in comparison to adjacent arenas and racetracks and parking lots. Aside from its former life as a cedar forest, the land beneath the sports complex has also been a burning dump, and for a while, the complex seemed haunted by the dump entombed beneath it. In the mid-1980s, playing football in the Meadowlands meant possibly risking your life, because shortly after the stadium opened, players for the Giants began developing cancer. By 1987, a running back had died of an inoperable brain tumor, another running back had died of cancer of the blood vessels, a twenty-seven-year-old offensive tackle had developed cancer of the lymph nodes, and another player had survived a bout of lymphoma. "Players complained of occasionally foul-smelling shower water, and the high incidence of leukemia in adjacent Rutherford . . ." *The Sporting News* reported. State officials assured people that before the stadium was built the garbage dump had been thoroughly covered with sand and soils "brought in from the outside" and that life had become more habitable for some creatures (the number of mammals found in the area has increased from six to seventeen since the first kickoff in 1978). One player asked to be traded, nonetheless. The mayor of East Rutherford, the town wherein the football stadium lies, said, "It seems to me to be more than a coincidence."

Cancer scares had faded by the time Dave and I canoed past the complex—no concrete links between the site and ill effects were ever discovered—and I offered this note as consolation to Dave as we glided beneath another highway bridge, the muscular steel supporting it dotted underneath with stalagmites of pigeon dung. We turned east into Peach Tree Island Creek. In a few seconds we came to a tide gate that blocked our path and we started to think about turning around. A duck swam by us that didn't look so much like a duck as a toxic chicken: its markings were mottled—black, red, and brown. I later learned it was an imported Muscovy duck, which apparently is an excellent meat bird, and that these ducks were being raised by a nearby family for food, but on the creek that day I didn't think that anyone would even live along Peach Tree Island Creek much less eat something that swam in it. And that was when Dave looked back toward an old dock around which the Muscovy ducks were paddling and said, "There's someone swimming over there."

The man swimming in Peach Tree Island Creek couldn't understand why I was asking him if he was concerned about water quality issues. "I mean, get real," he said, in a thick Romanian accent. He was big and heavyset and he wore a black, bikini brief–style bathing suit. He repeated the phrase "get real" several times. "I put it this way to you," he continued. "If the police told me to get out, then I would, but I would get back in. Anyway, the guy who owns the property had a sign. It was in Arabic because he is Muslim, and it said, 'Swimming here.' "

Dave was steadying the canoe in the water as I was listening to the man speak.

"For two years, I didn't swim here at all," he went on. "For a while, I was scared, but I see the owner swim here and he has no effects. If I had effects, I would not go in any longer. I mean, I break ice in river where I am from and I go in and I feel great. The people tell me that the water is no good here, but they are there and I am here. Here it is fine. I mean, *get real!* When the tide is high, it is very nice. When the tide is low, the water doesn't look so good and then I don't go in. That's simple. I could go to Sandy Hook or to Coney Island, but it's far away. Here, I am five minutes away from my home. And besides, one day I go into water in Coney Island and I get out and I have a big rash. A big rash all over! I had to go to doctor. He gave me some kind of antibiotic. But it's okay. Really. I mean, we have fish here. You should see the fish jump."

"What kind of fish?" I asked him.

"I wouldn't know," he said.

In retrospect, we should have turned around when we had the chance, but we held out hope of finding a passage back to the Hackensack until the very last minute. We had pulled the canoe up over the tide gate, with difficulty. Dave had scouted ahead to discover that Peach Tree Island Creek continued on the other side but only for a dozen or so yards, where it came to another tide gate and a tunnel beneath a street, so we decided to portage the canoe for that dozen yards, and we put in again just past the second gate, near the corporate offices of Donna Karan, the New York fashion designer. At this point, it still seemed conceivable that we might find a way to canoe through the swamps to the Hackensack River. Then again, part of the reason it still seemed conceivable was because we didn't really have a backup plan.

When we put in this time, we eased the canoe into a soupy brown liquid across from a toxic clean-up site—a piece of property covered with plastic and vented with fans—and then paddled as quickly as we could without stirring up the root beer–colored water. We were using the radio towers ahead of us as our guide, along with our compass and our maps, but the creek began to take uncharted turns. We were beginning to feel lost again. The banks of the creek were now more wooded, and soon there were more creeks and more ditches and too many navigational choices and the woods began to seem darker until finally I had no idea where to turn or whether one rheumy little body of water would lead us to a dead end where we would have no further opportunities for portage. It was then that I saw something dark and big and slime covered up in the distance. It walked up out of the creek and up a bank and off into the woods. It was either a giant muskrat or a wild dog or maybe some mutated version of the two.

I was a little frantic now, and Dave agreed then and there that we should take to land, so we yanked the canoe out of the water beneath a sign marked HAZARDOUS and up into the parking lot of some kind of a warehouse. We figured we were approximately one mile west of the Hackensack and approximately a quarter of a mile from any road. We were also hot and exhausted and running low on supplies such as drinking water (water filtering was just totally out of the question). Standing there in our life jackets, poring over our maps as we stood next to our big red canoe, we didn't know what to do.

When we saw a security guard approaching in his security vehicle, I thought we might be arrested for trespassing or at least questioned, but he looked at us and didn't seem to pause—as if stranded canoeists were an everyday occurrence on the banks of Meadowlands creeks. Dave and I did a double take, and then I ran after the security guard and asked if we could pay him to carry our canoe to water in the back of his security vehicle, which was a small white Toyota pickup truck. He agreed. Dave sat in the truck bed holding down the canoe as we drove down a highway and the canoe attempted to escape in the wind; I sat in the front seat in the air-conditioning. The security guard, whose name was Ed, turned his truck's yellow flashing lights on. People honked at us, upset that we were going too slow. In a couple of minutes, Ed dropped us off at a marina / driving range / restaurant on the Hackensack River at the dead end of Paterson Plank Road. We were directly across the river from where we had started out that morning. We thanked Ed profusely. Ed was our Sacagawea.

I pulled out some cash.

"Don't worry about it," Ed said.

At the marina / driving range / restaurant, we bought some Gatorade and I took in the panorama of our trip that day while Dave hit golf balls off toward the natural gas pipeline that is right out where the driving range turns from lawn to swamp grass. A little while later, we crossed the Hackensack back to where our car was parked. When we did, it was low tide and we got stuck in the muck.

Valley of
the Garbage Hills

THERE ARE REAL HILLS IN THE MEADOWLANDS AND THERE ARE
garbage hills. The real hills are outnumbered by the garbage
hills. Snake Hill and the lesser Little Snake Hill, which is just
across the New Jersey Turnpike from Snake Hill, are the only
real hills. The rest of the hills are garbage hills. Garbage hills are
everywhere in the meadows, and they are filled with all different types of garbage. Many are filled with household garbage.
For a long time, the Meadowlands was the largest garbage dump
in the world. In the 1970s, eleven thousand tons of garbage were
dumped there every day—an amount that would just about fill
Giants Stadium. The trash was piled high into hills; it was spread
out across the marshes. Today, most of these hills have grown
covers of grass and phragmites and wormwood and as a result
they are soft little rolling hills; if you didn't know better, you

might guess they were formed by a glacier. Still other hills are filled with the garbage of the construction industry. If you put a shovel into the ground and dig just about anywhere in the Meadowlands, it won't be long until you hit rubble from a building that was once somewhere else. In Kearny, one old dump contains pieces of what was once Europe. In 1941, under the auspices of the Lend-Lease Act, shipments of defense equipment went from the United States to Great Britain by boat. On their return trip, the boats used rubble from London bombings as ballast. William Keegan, a Kearny dump owner, contracted to accept the ballast. As a result, some of the hills of the Kearny Meadows are London hills.

In general, the garbage hills stank. When particular hills smelled especially bad, dump workers were charged with spraying the hills with disinfectant, usually mint scented. On such occasions, great swarms of roaches reacted violently. "Don't ever let anybody tell you that roaches can't fly, because I've seen 'em fly," an old dump worker told me once. A lot of the dumps were run by the Mob, which leased land throughout the Meadowlands. Dumps under the Mob's jurisdiction often accepted chemical waste for disposal that wasn't accepted elsewhere. This was good for the people who wanted to get rid of chemical wastes, and it was good for the Mob. When the Mob wanted something to disappear completely, they dumped it in pools of acid in the Meadowlands. In general, the Mob-affiliated dumps tended to be lax with regard to the few environmental regulations that existed in those days, and if loose garbage began to blow off a dump, then the rest of the offending loose garbage on the dump was usually accidentally burned. Fires often ended up burning out of control so that underground fires were common in the Meadowlands; methane gas within the old dumps fueled the flames, and the layers after layers of decomposed vegetation that make up the meadow floor served as tinder. Fire trucks raced out between the dumps on dirt roads that were overgrown with reeds and, at night, bumpy with scurrying rats. Fire trucks often ran out of water in the middle of the swamp; at low tide, they couldn't even pump from the polluted creeks. The dump that was where Giants Stadium is now burned constantly for several years. *The Passaic Herald-News* referred to it variously as "stench-laden" and as a "stinking pall of smoke." Tons of sand from the bottom of New York Harbor finally put that fire out. Underground fires are still common today in the Meadowlands, and if you walk along some of the old hills or look out at them through train windows you can see little black holes where the hills have recently burped hot gases or fire.

Once in a great while, the dumps accidentally revealed treasures. The old dump workers have stories about old coins they found, about discovering rare objects of all different sorts, but people generally seem to overestimate the market value of what might be in the Meadowlands' garbage hills. "I'll bet you there's more gold in there than anywhere," a dump worker told me. "Can you imagine what people throw away by accident?" another one said. "They threw a lot of antiques in those dumps back then, because they had no idea how much that stuff was gonna be worth today." A dump worker once confided to me that he thinks of the old dumps not so much as huge piles of garbage or as burial mounds of decaying junk, but as the resting place of the lost baseball cards of his childhood and the childhood of his boyhood New Jersey friends. When more of the dumps were active, it was not unusual for a non–dump worker to suddenly drive up to a dump in his or her car and dig through trash at random, vainly searching for a winning lottery ticket that was accidentally discarded. There are a few legendary discoveries. A lot of the old dump workers tell of the day that one of their colleagues struck an old coffee can while operating a bulldozer. No one ever actually saw the coffee can; they only saw a little cloud of paper currency hover over the hill. The dump worker who struck the can immediately abandoned his bulldozer and sprinted down the garbage hill to his home in Lyndhurst. It is said that he bought a new house and never worked again.

The big difference between the garbage hills and the real hills in the Meadowlands is that the garbage hills are alive. In some completely peopleless areas of the swamp, there are billions of microscopic organisms thriving underground in dark, oxygen-free communities. They multiply and even evolve so that they can more readily digest the trash at their disposal. It can take a team of three organisms to finish off a dump-buried particle of cellulose in a bit of newspaper too small to even see. Eventually, there are whole suites of organisms in each hill as if each hill were a bacterial high-rise. After having ingested the tiniest portion of leftover New Jersey or New York, these cells then exhale huge underground plumes of carbon dioxide and of warm moist methane, giant stillborn tropical winds that seep through the ground to feed the Meadowlands' fires, or creep up into the atmosphere, where they eat away at the Earth-protecting layer of ozone. When you gaze at a garbage hill, you have to imagine a shadow hill hiding inside, a hill that closely follows the profile of the garbage hill except that it is slightly lower and thinner and that it is made mostly of water. And then there is the water—water that comes in from the sky, water that comes in on the arriving trash, water that mingles with the bacteria and the trash, and in the end transubstantiates into what is known in the landfill business as leachate, a garbage juice. When the slope of the hidden hill of water rises to meet the level of the visible garbage hill, a tiny leachate spring forms, a seep. By one estimate, a little over a billion gallons of leachate flows forth each year from out of the twenty-five hundred acres of old landfills in the Meadowlands.

One afternoon I drove back through a field of abandoned cars and walked along the edge of a garbage hill, a forty-foot drumlin of compacted trash that owed its topography to the waste of the city of Newark. On the side of the scraggly grass-covered hill, little black patches were scars from a recent fire. There had been rain the night before, so it wasn't long before I found a little leachate seep, a black ooze trickling down the slope of the hill, an espresso of refuse. In a few hours, this stream would find its way down into the already spoiled groundwater of the Meadowlands; it would mingle with toxic streams, and perhaps dilute whatever rare drop of water in the region might somehow be without the trace of humankind. But in this moment, here at its birth, at a stream's source in the modern meadows, this little seep was pure pollution, a pristine stew of oil and grease, of cyanide and arsenic, of cadmium, chromium, copper, lead, nickel, silver, mercury, and zinc. I touched this fluid—my fingertip was a bluish caramel color—and it was warm and fresh. A few yards away, where the stream collected into a benzene-scented pool, a mallard swam alone.

Through the fifties, and well into the sixties and seventies, the Meadowlands continued to be trashed. The skyline in those years featured trash-fat gulls and Dantean clouds of smoke and bulldozers that fed the insatiable fires. Untreated sewage spilled into the waterways. Some underground fires burned out of control for decades. The towns that comprise the

Meadowlands squabbled over plans to end dumping, while people who considered the battered wetlands to be without any ecological value continued to dump. Then, in 1968, the state legislature created the Hackensack Meadowlands Development Commission, which was charged with developing the Meadowlands and cleaning them up. To handle all the trash, the HMDC initially considered constructing the world's largest incinerator, but environmentalists protested. In 1973, the HMDC settled on a large-scale recycling program, and later, instead of building the world's largest incinerator, it built the world's largest trash baler. In 1982, as proof of its intention to stop dumping, the HMDC located its headquarters on land situated between a dump in Lyndhurst and the Kingsland Marsh, which, until the HMDC moved there, was the proposed site of yet another dump. Soon, the dumps began shutting down. While the municipalities dealt with the courts, the staff of the HMDC began to meet with local dump owners. Meetings with the non-Mob-affiliated dump owners generally went well. Meetings with the Mob-affiliated owners were more unpredictable. Several late-night meetings took place at the scenes of burning dumps. One HMDC staff member tells the story of being chased by a black Town Car through the streets of Hackensack. Another tells about the time a dump owner brought his wife with him to HMDC headquarters for a 10 A.M. meeting. The dump owner's wife was wearing a mink coat and more diamonds than are commonly worn amid the dumps in the Meadowlands. When she sat down at the table of arch-eyebrowed state bureaucrats, she said, "I gotta get comfortable," and, in so doing, slapped down her revolver on the table.

Today, people continue to dump illegally—as if it were recreational—but only one dump is officially open, and every day the Meadowlands legally receives 1,450 tons of trash. This official trash is primarily the responsibility of two people: Tom Marturano, a thickly built man with a strong voice and a hearty laugh, who parks his truck behind a little sign that says, RESERVED FOR THE DIRECTOR OF SOLID WASTE, and Chris Dour, a solid waste engineer for the HMDC, who is tall and thin and sits at a desk down the hall from Marturano's beneath a poster that exclaims, "GARBAGE IS BEAUTIFUL." Marturano's office has a view of the Saw Mill Wildlife Refuge, of the western spur of the New Jersey Turnpike, and of this last open dump, a one-hundred-and-thirty-foot-tall four-hundred-acre mountain that, through decomposition, sinks down five feet every year under its own weight. This hill is officially referred to as the Balefill Site and unofficially known as Mount Arlington, a name derived from that fact that it is located on what was once a meadow in North Arlington. Technically, it is only supposed to receive Bergen County trash, but when individuals or groups in the vicinity of New York are having difficulties disposing of something, they generally end up negotiating with Marturano. A tractor trailer load of spoiled peanut butter showed up at Mount Arlington recently, as well as crates of spices that were spicy but didn't pass inspection somewhere. Two years ago, Marturano consented to the delivery of a warehouseful of garlic that had spoiled over the course of a summer— he called in men wearing special suits with breathing apparatus to execute the transfer. A while back the state police called looking to make a reservation on Mount Arlington for a headless whale. "It was four-thirty on a Friday afternoon," Marturano remembered recently, as he pointed out to Mount Arlington, "and the guy from the state police said, 'Is your landfill open tomorrow?' And I said, 'Yeah.' And he said, 'Good. We're bringing down a whale.' And I said, 'What do you mean, you're bringing down a whale?' And he said a whale got hit in Newark Bay." I remember, it came in three parts. It was forty-five feet long and it weighed twenty-three tons. The rats and seagulls, boy, they feasted that day." A few months before the whale arrived, Marturano became enraged when a local animal control official sent the bodies of dogs to the landfill after they had been gassed. As it turned out, the animal control officer wasn't using enough gas, and the all-but-dead dogs were seen on the great garbage hill occasionally moving and even walking around.

Chris Dour drove me through solid waste operations once. We drove first to the baler, and along the way, Dour said, "As a kid, I used to come down here to the dumps for junkyard parts, and I'd be standing there looking at the guys on top of the dumps and saying, 'Who the hell is doing that?' And then, of course, I was working here four years later." The baler is a giant trash compactor that does its work in an airplane hangarlike building where piles of stinking garbage patiently wait their turn. "That's maybe about a thousand tons of garbage," Dour said, as we looked out on the floor. A man operated the baler from inside a glass booth hanging in the rafters. A rat, perched nearby, watched with interest. The facility smelled like garbage. "To me, it's never so bad that it really bothers me to come in here," Dour said, "but one time I was behind a truckload of fish that was coming in from a fish market and it was unbelievable. But then again, I was on top when there was a truckload of cologne thrown up there. It was short-weighted, I think. The landfill smelled great that day." As Dour spoke, the baler, with long mechanical grunts, transformed the floor's anarchy into one-ton cubes. "It's pretty compact, as opposed to what it used to be," Dour said. "In the old days, they'd muck out the peat and the mud in the Meadowlands, put the garbage in the water, light a match, and leave. Now nobody in their right mind would put a landfill in wetlands."

We followed the cubes up to the top of Mount Arlington, along the route for trucks carrying unregulated medical waste. On top of the Balefill Landfill, there are two roads with street signs and names. We passed a street called Nature's Choice, which is where yard debris is dumped, composted, and carted away again. It was like a little planned garbage community. In a few minutes, we came to a football-field-sized clearing one hundred and thirty feet in the air. Giant tractors were setting the compacted trash cubes into the hill as seagulls cheered them on. It was a perfectly clear spring day, so Dour got out of the car and walked on the earthlike garbage and enjoyed the view, which encompassed the Meadowlands and its towns and New York and Newark Bay and New York Harbor. I set my foot down and took one small step and the ground felt soft but firm. Dour pointed out a couple of toxic cleanup sites in the distance, one where oil had been poured over acres and acres of wetland, and one in a marsh where a huge chunk of New Jersey's Watchung Mountains was disposed of after being removed to make way for an interstate highway. As Dour spoke, the loose trash at our feet was blowing in tiny whirlpools in the wind. "Sometimes, we get calls from people who want to film up here," Dour said. "Once, we got a call from Bette Midler's husband's production crew. I think that's who it was. They wanted to set up tables on top of the landfill for breakfast or something for a special on HBO. Then I think they realized it was kind of a bad idea. Another time somebody was doing a futuristic movie. It was about a future where races were being pitted against each other, or something along those lines, and basically we said no, because the commission didn't really want to be a part of anything like that."

As opposed to the older garbage hills in the Meadowlands, the modern garbage hills are maintained, and when we got back in his Jeep, Dour drove us off from where the workers were hill manufacturing, to a point on Mount Arlington where we could see its respiratory system. In the grassy areas, pipes stuck out of the ground every few dozen yards, each a way station in the HMDC's experimental methane collection program. Long perforated pipes run into the hill and mine its methane gas, which is used to heat local homes. Across a highway, we saw an old landfill being lined and surrounded with a kind of clay moat, in an effort to prevent leachate leakage. "We try to create a clay bathtub," Dour said. Geology helps in this endeavor in that the bottom of the Meadowlands is clay. A few of the already lined landfills' leachate collection systems run directly to local sewage treatment plants. The leachate collection systems on other landfills are not connected to anything, though, and they must be manually emptied, like landfill colostomy bags. This is the case with one lined dump in south Kearny, a forty-foot pile near the Kearny Marsh. A truck visits the old dump two times each day to pump it out and then drives a few blocks away where the truck driver pulls up a manhole cover and pumps the leachate into a sewer line, which in turn takes the leachate to a sewage treatment plant. Generally, this works without a hitch. But recently the truck driver drove to the landfill, withdrew his leachate deposit, and then attempted to save time by transferring the leachate into the local sewer line at a faster rate than usual. As it turned out, the sewer line couldn't handle so much so fast and within minutes some of the people living in homes near the manhole cover were surprised to see leachate welling up in their sinks and toilet bowls.

*   *   *

Anthony Malanka is a dump owner I know who operates the Malanka Mall Landfill. The Malanka dump, as his site is known, is on the shore of the Hackensack River in Secaucus, in between Snake Hill and Little Snake Hill. His offices are in Union City, on the top of a ridge that looks down into the Meadowlands. Malanka is president of a business founded by his grandfather, who emigrated from Italy in 1890 and began his life in the New World carting garbage. As a young man, Malanka worked in the dumps, which were then run by his father, but the garbage business never appealed to him the way it did to the rest of his family, so after serving in Korea he struck out for a while and ran a diner in Secaucus that was located alongside vegetable farms and catered to truck drivers. When the diner closed, Malanka returned to landfill operations. Since then, his landfill has been closed up and his relatives have mostly passed away, and for a while now he has dreamed of liquidating his operations. Until he does, he sits up in his empty suite of old offices—he sold all the garbage trucks and all the office furniture, except for a desk and a phone—and he takes calls from the occasional prospective buyer. Malanka is only five feet ten but you can tell that he played guard on his college football team and that he used to easily put away ten eggs at a time in eating contests in the army. "All I have keeping me here are the buildings and a couple of lawsuits," he told me one day, just after he pulled up to his office from his home in Secaucus. "I'd sell the building, but who's gonna buy this? And as far as the landfill goes, do you want it? I'll give it to you. I've been trying to retire since I was sixty. Now I'm sixty-seven. I mean, basically, I'm just sitting here paying for the sins of my family."

Tony Malanka visits his old dump every day to make certain it is free of trash and litter, rolling his eyes at the irony of dump cleaning. "They make you maintain it until perpetuity and all that shit," he says, as he drives his car down into the Meadowlands. The dump he visits actually consists of two dumps—one seventy-foot-tall hill, the other fifty feet tall. Each has sunk down about twenty feet into the swamp in as many years. The other day as Malanka drove his car back along some gravel and up the little dirt road that leads to his garbage hill, he said, "Now they call 'em sanitary landfills. Before, we called them dumps. You dug a hole, you threw garbage in it, you burned it, and you covered it up. If you didn't cover it, there'd be seagulls all over. They said that affected the airports. I'm not really sure." He shoved his hands deep into the pockets of his long gray raincoat. "I like coming here, to tell you the truth," Malanka said, with the New Jersey Turnpike at his back and a reed-filled area of creeks and mosquito channels before him. "It's always an adventure. But look at this . . ." He picked up a piece of trash, and motioned toward some workers doing railroad construction. "I'm working all the time to keep this place clean, I'll tell you," he continued. "I was out here with my wife the other day picking up garbage, and I was kidding her. Last week we were a swinging couple in Atlantic City. Then, the next day we're watching our grandkids, and now we're out here in our old clothes picking up trash on a dump."

Close to the top of his fifty-foot dump, Malanka reminisced about wildlife. Some of the dump workers made soup from giant turtles, others kept pheasants in a cage. The construction foreman used to fill the back of his truck with rabbits. Rats were everywhere. "Let's put it this way," Malanka said, regarding rats. "They weren't shy." Today, there are numerous pheasants and songbirds that Malanka doesn't bother to identify. "Basically, what I'm doing is running a wildlife sanctuary here," he likes to say. He recalled a time when people would visit the dump looking for lost items. "People used to call up all the time and say, 'I lost my jewels,' and we'd let 'em come down and look around. The best one was some friggin' law firm or something threw out all the wrong files and what I got a kick out of was then they came down here all dressed up. They took their jackets off and started to dig."

As we stood on Malanka's dump, someone suddenly fired a gun. I jumped. Malanka waved his hand, dismissing the blast. "There's a shooting range over there," he said. "I use this place as a shooting range myself. As a matter of fact, I have a little pistol I like to take out, and the other day when I was out here with my wife, I let her give it a try and she knocked off three bottles the first time. It took me a year and a half to hit one. I couldn't believe it."

We drove down off the dump and back to Union City, where we had a lunch at Louis', an Italian restaurant. The interior was dark with red walls and lots of candles and hanging lanterns. We sat down and ordered some pasta, some red wine, and some sausage on the side. Malanka told the story of the day he fell into the blood-and-guts-filled trench outside a North Bergen slaughterhouse, when as a child he was at a picnic and fetching his baseball. "People were standing away from me for days afterward. I mean, I stunk," he said. "And I remember, we came right here to this place for dinner. Nobody wanted to sit next to me." As Malanka was telling this story, the mayor of a Meadowlands-area municipality came into the restaurant and passed our table. He reached down and grabbed Malanka's hand and shook it. Malanka never looked up. When the mayor sat down, Malanka whispered that the mayor's town owed Malanka money from when Malanka & Sons was still carting garbage. Malanka shook his head. "I can't believe that guy has the nerve to shake my hand," Malanka said. "What a jerk."

Finally, the pasta and the sausage arrived. Malanka looked at the plate of sausage with disgust.

I asked him what was wrong.

"Look at it!" he said. "It's burned!" He was practically shouting. He speared the sausage disdainfully with his fork and raised it into the air. He said, "What is this, a turd?"

I volunteered to eat it; it looked okay to me.

Malanka would not hear of it. He called over the waiter. "What is this, a turd?" he said again, this time to the waiter. "Hey, are you listening to me?"

The waiter nodded his head.

"Good," Malanka continued. "Well, let me tell you something. If my wife served me this, first of all, I wouldn't eat it. But if my wife gave me that sausage, let me tell you something, I'd divorce her. Do you hear me? I'd *divorce* her!"

Malanka looked at me again and said, "What is this, a turd?"

Skeeters

PUBLIC DISTASTE FOR THE MEADOWLANDS IS NOT A MODERN phenomenon; the area has always been abhorred by travelers. The Meadowlands owes its longtime reputation as one of the most disgusting areas in America mostly to three things: trash, industry, and mosquitoes. The impression of the Meadowlands as toxically overindustrialized is relatively recent compared to its reputation as a giant mosquito-breeding ground. People have been complaining about mosquitoes in the Meadowlands since New York City was first settled. The early Dutch settlers of the area described mosquitoes as big as sparrows. When people crossed the meadows on horseback in the 1700s, they often waited a day or two in Newark for the horse to "blood up." Farmers who kept slaves on the farms of the Meadowlands used mosquitoes as a means of punishment; slaves were shackled and left in areas where mosquitoes were known to swarm. Many slaves died after being left out on the meadows. The mosquito situation continued well into the twentieth century. Sometimes factories on the meadows closed down during a hatch. In 1914, passengers waiting in a Newark train station on a summer day said they couldn't see the station's walls. One of the most famous references to mosquitoes in the Meadowlands was composed by Henry Wansey, an eighteenth-century British traveler. In 1765, he wrote, "All the way to Newark . . . is a very flat, marshy country, intersected with rivers, [and] many cedar swamps, abounding with mosquitoes, which bit our legs and hands exceedingly; where they fix they will continue sucking our blood if not disturbed, till they swell to four times their ordinary size, when they absolutely fall off and burst from their fullness." The man who did the most to combat the mosquito problem in the Meadowlands was John B. Smith, America's first great mosquito warrior.

Smith was born John Schmidt in 1858 to German immigrants in Brooklyn, where as a young man, he joined his first insect club and drew praise for his highly detailed beetle illustrations. (Though he would eventually be known for his work with mosquitoes, he would always have a soft spot for beetles, and upon his death a colleague wrote, "To the end of his life he kept constantly in touch with the beetle men.") Smith studied law and clerked at a law firm and even passed the bar in 1879, but his heart was with insects. In comparing law and entomology, he used to say, "A fly on the wall is more interesting than a case in hand." Shortly after 1884, in a burst of passion, he quit his job; proposed to his wife-to-be, Marie von Meske; and took a job as special agent in the bureau of entomology at the U.S. Department of Agriculture, where he worked until 1889, when he was made professor of entomology at Rutgers. A few years later, he was appointed New Jersey State Entomologist. It was his dream job. He was soon supervising insect investigations and composing long entomological reports with titles such as "Remedy for Onion Maggot," "Is the Woodpecker Useful?," and "An Experience with Rose Bugs." He worked at the Agricultural College Experiment Station at Rutgers, where he dictated all his work to Augusta von Meske, stenographer and typist for the experiment station and Smith's mother-in-law.

Sitting at his desk, the microscope on his right hand always at the ready and the walls of his office decorated with pin-splayed insects—his collection of thirty thousand owlet moths was renowned—John B. Smith was the picture of entomological determination. He was tall and stout—"a vigorous, bushy-bearded genius," was how a colleague once described him—and his mustache spread out like the wings of a dragonfly from beneath a big, bulbous nose. He considered himself an entomologist of the world; his library held foreign titles such as *Insects Abroad* and *The Genitalia of the British Museum.* At Rutgers, he was considered the most popular professor on campus—he and his wife were known for their parties. He was the kind of guy who would run into a lab during a fire to retrieve insect specimens while the firemen warned him away or he would take it upon himself to spray the campus elm trees for insects in his spare time. His motto was, "Every hour has its task, every moment has an opportunity." He seized his moment of opportunity as an entomologist by applying insect science to everyday pursuits, such as agriculture. His book *Our Insect Friends and Enemies* became a standard at agricultural colleges. In 1900, Smith read *Mosquitoes,* a book by L. O. Howard, his former boss at the Department of Agriculture. The book documented the mosquito's threat to public health and prescribed methods of mosquito extermination, and it changed John Smith's life. From that moment on, Smith became the prophet for a mosquito-free New Jersey, and America.

To people living at the turn of the century, mosquitoes were nothing more than a terrible nuisance, and the idea that they could transmit deadly disease was inconceivable. Scientists thought you contracted malaria or yellow fever when you inhaled bad air. (Malaria comes from the Italian words *mal* and *aria,* which together mean bad air.) Swamp air was high on the bad air list. Swamp air was thought to derive its diseased potency from sewage pools and stews of decaying life. A few people theorized that mosquitoes might have *something* to do with disease and subsequently proposed mosquito control tactics. In 1882, Dr. Albert Freeman Africanus King, a professor of obstetrics, who was the first physician to attend to Lincoln after he was shot, proposed that the city of Washington, D.C., be encircled by a giant wire screen built to the height of the Washington Monument. But there was no proof of the mosquito's role as disease carrier until 1897, when Ronald Ross, an English physician working in a remote field hospital in Secunderabad, India, cut open a mosquito that had just bitten a patient infected with malaria and put it under a microscope. Ross observed the malarial parasite in the mosquito's intestinal tract. Ross was a poet and on the evening of his discovery, he wrote the only poem he would ever publish, which went, in part, like this:

> *I know this little thing*
> *A myriad men will save.*
> *O Death, where is thy sting?*
> *Thy victory, O Grave.*

The subsequent discovery of the mosquito's transmission of yellow fever was the subject of *Yellow Jack,* a play that dramatized the work of Dr. Walter Reed, a U.S. Army physician who combated the fever in Cuba. To prove that malaria could not be contracted any other way, Reed and his men slept in hospital wards in the dirty bed sheets and soiled clothes of yellow fever patients. L. O. Howard's book summarized all that was known to date about mosquitoes and their disease-carrying abilities and then suggested means by which the mosquito might be annihilated—primarily by draining swamps and marshes. As Smith read *Mosquito,* he must have thought, *Eureka!* In Newark alone, hundreds of people died every year from the diseases of the swamp. (There were also yellow fever epidemics in Louisiana and Tennessee, and the deaths that resulted from an outbreak of yellow fever in 1798 are thought to have caused Philadelphia to fall from its position as number one American port.) The mosquito took its toll agriculturally as well: in New Jersey, milk production suffered because of great numbers of mosquitoes biting cows. With L. O. Howard's broad battle plan in hand, Smith quickly sent out letters throughout the state announcing his intention to eliminate what had become known nationally as New Jersey's state bird.

To say there was not a groundswell of public support for the elimination of mosquitoes is putting it mildly. When he told the state legislature that the southern portion of New Jersey, undeveloped and ruled by mosquitoes at the time, would one day be habitable, the legislators laughed at him. He wrote that people treated his ideas as if they were "a huge joke." One editorial cartoonist drew Smith wearing a halo of mosquitoes, each stinging him with a wisecrack. Smith pressed on with his crusade undaunted, inspired by the conviction that humankind was at war with the blood-sucking bug. He identified thirty-three types of mosquitoes in New Jersey. He bred mosquitoes from all over the state in his office, each specimen arranged by size; a reporter for *The Newark Sunday Call* described his workplace as "a veritable mosquito ranch." Smith showed up at the

St. Louis Exposition with a huge display that, among other things, illustrated the life cycle of the mosquito; he buzzed to passersby about mosquito reductions that could be achieved not just in New Jersey but nationwide. Smith made important mosquito findings, such as the discovery that swarms of the salt marsh mosquito, the *Aedes solicitan,* can travel as far as forty miles from where they were bred. He concentrated his studies on the *Aedes solicitan,* which was also known to entomologists as the Jersey Mosquito. He came to know this creature intimately, so that when he died and a group of entomologists held a dinner in his honor, they raised their glasses and toasted him as the world's greatest authority on *Aedes solicitan.* In a few years, public opinion turned around. Smith became known more affectionately as Jersey's Mosquito Sharp. *The Newark Evening News* now drew him flying on a mosquito in their cartoons. He was like a pest that didn't go away.

The biggest casualty in John B. Smith's war against the mosquito was the Meadowlands. Beginning in 1904, in order to eliminate the mosquito, Smith began draining the Newark meadows. His idea was to turn the swamps and marshes from a place where water pooled haphazardly, where it eddied and puddled and offered salt marsh mosquitos infinite breeding opportunities, into a giant dish-draining board, a place where water would never be still, never pause, where it would have opportunity only to drain away. To do this, Smith hired gangs of men to dig ditches all over the meadows by tractorlike machine or by hand, sometimes using shovels that required two men. Digging ditches by hand was backbreaking work, and, while working, the diggers sang songs that went like this:

> *Bend your knees, straighten out,*
> *Something's got to give,*

It's either the sod or your back,
See which one will live.

If a ditchdigger's back didn't break, then he might suffer otherwise, because the salt hay farmers who were still operating profitably at the time didn't appreciate the state entomologist cutting ditches through their fields—they were likely to threaten ditchdiggers with guns. Nonetheless, Smith had drained forty-five hundred acres within a short time. "The result of this experiment was very successful," he wrote, "and rendered into a dry surface with no standing water a section of the meadow that, before draining, was a quagmire." To complement the ditches, Smith directed the construction of dikes on the meadows to control tidewater. Any remaining ponds were filled with gambusia, a fish that devoured young mosquitoes, and a thin film of oil was sprayed across acres and acres of the Meadowlands to smother mosquito larvae in the water before they ever had a chance to fly. In the midst of all his experimentation, Smith was never too busy to take influential New Jerseyans out in boats on the meadows to show off his work. On one trip, he stopped his boat as it approached a work site and took a vial of citronella from one of the many pockets of his big coat. "One moment, gentlemen," he said. "I think we shall all be the better for a little of this. It's a newly discovered mosquito repellent." The men watched as Smith covered his arm with the yellowish liquid and then plunged it into a small squadron of *solicitans*. "Look," he said, and the boatload of spectators gasped as the mosquitoes all flew away.

With the apparent success of his work on the Newark meadows, Smith became a national celebrity, advising mosquito control officials all over the United States. He was asked to contribute articles to periodicals ranging from *Popular Sci-*

ence Monthly to *The Book Lovers Magazine.* When mosquitos threatened the completion of construction of the Panama Canal, editorials called for Smith with the refrain: "Send Jersey's Mosquito Man." Smith traveled the world observing mosquito control procedures in the Netherlands, Germany, France, and Hungary. When he died, he was only a few days away from seeing the centerpiece of his antimosquito plan put in place: a law making mosquito control mandatory in every county in New Jersey (a law that would later be copied by every state in the United States). Shortly before the legislation went up for the vote, Smith, who was fifty-three at the time, took sick with Bright's disease. He continued to work in all his posts. "I wish to die in the harness," he told people. He didn't quit his job until a month before his death in 1912. Up until the end, students brought papers to his home. Editorial writers across the state mourned his passing. "In the war of the Mosquito, Professor John B. Smith, who died yesterday, gave a great part of his life to making the lives of the citizens of New Jersey bearable," one newspaper wrote. On the day he was buried, Governor Woodrow Wilson signed his mosquito control bill. At the time of Smith's death, it was estimated that he was responsible for 3,814,974 feet of ditches.

Mosquito control officials in New Jersey and all over America still speak in awe of John B. Smith (even if his ditches, in extinguishing the saltwater mosquito problem, actually *increased* the number of freshwater mosquitoes in the Meadowlands). And his legacy is etched into the face of the Meadowlands. Hundreds of his ditches intersect all the creeks and the rivers like capillaries in a hungover eye. Before I ever knew what they were, in the days when I would try to imagine whether they were man-made or natural, I thought of them the way people once thought about canals on Mars.

*　　　　*　　　　*

John B. Smith's dream of a mosquito-free New Jersey is still alive in some ways, and the person in charge of executing that dream on the Meadowlands today is Leonard Soccio, chief inspector in the mosquito control division of the Bergen County Department of Public Works. Soccio's office is on the side of a big old garage that is tucked away in some woods next to a park in Paramus. He is a short, stocky man with a neatly trimmed mustache, thinning gray hair, a kind face, and arms thick from years of hard work in the ditches of the Meadowlands. He is intimate with the Meadowlands not just because he has been employed by the commission for the past thirty-seven years but also because he worked on area dumps before that and recreated in the Meadowlands even before that (his name is one of the many spray-painted on the side of Snake Hill). The last time I saw him, on a warm spring afternoon, he said to me, "As far as the mosquito people go, I'm pretty much the last of the Mohicans."

When Soccio began working in mosquito control, the mosquitoes in the Meadowlands were a lot worse than they are today. There were still strong pockets of resistance on the meadows, little guerrilla mosquito forces. "In the old days, we had areas where we had to spray just to get in," he said. The swarms weren't the black clouds of historic times, but they were swarms, and the way you could tell you were in the midst of one was that all of a sudden you would look down and see your entire body covered with mosquitoes, each poised to bite. There were men and ditch digging machines at work in the meadows all year round. "We had a regular hard labor gang there," Soccio said. In the fifties and sixties, the mosquito commission began using DDT and other pesticides, and the Meadowlands were first sprayed from the air with a biplane piloted by a man wearing a long white scarf. On the ground, mosquito workers sometimes had to wade through trash, and one man drowned in Berry's Creek Canal. In Soccio's office are old pictures of him working with various chemicals and sprays. In one, he is standing astride a hole as another worker pumps cyanide into it—Soccio was helping out with a Meadowlands' rat problem. "If the wind had blown the wrong way, that stuff would have been up my nose. I would have been lying there like a rat," he said. He shook his head and grimaced. "Here's another one with me spraying DDT. *Christ!* I used to swim in that crap."

Soccio's operation would please John B. Smith. "Today, you got integrated control," Soccio explained proudly. "You got your chemical, your biological, and you got your abatement." Abatement involves controlling the flow of the creeks in the Meadowlands, most named for farmers or landowners or people and places no one can recall anymore: Muddabuck Creek, Doctor Creek, and a creek that's known as the West Riser Ditch in Moonachie. With regard to biological warfare, the commission relies primarily on gambusia, which are stocked in pools of still water. It also operates numerous mosquito surveillance traps throughout the meadows: there are traps that draw mosquitoes with lightbulbs, traps that draw them by a live pigeon protected from bites in a screened container (Soccio stressed that no pigeons are harmed in the course of the commission's work). In the lightbulb trap, a light lures the mosquito, a fan makes the capture, and poison neutralizes it. "*Pipiens* love it," Soccio said, referring to *Culex pipiens,* a prevalent species. Mosquitoes that are taken alive are escorted to the commission's refrigerator, a standard residential model. "We put 'em in the refrigerator and knock 'em down for a couple of hours and then count 'em," he said. "One time we counted three thousand. And that's not an unusual number."

Taxonomic diagrams of each species of mosquito decorate Soccio's old office wall like wanted posters in a post office. In general, the gang that infests the Meadowlands and its environs is composed of females—male mosquitoes are of no consequence to the commission because they do not sting—and they have as their motive the nourishment of their eggs, which are deposited in the various types of Meadowlands water. The mosquito gets its blood with what is technically a long beak, known to entomologists as its proboscis, which it unfurls from its sheath to penetrate the skin of its victim and execute the blood heist. The proboscis itself is like a sophisticated microscopic oil drilling rig: it contains six separate tubes and stylets. As the proboscis enters the victim, it begins searching for the blood supply. The proboscis is withdrawn and reinserted, exploring in the fleshy dark until it discovers a capillary, and then bends and stretches to follow the course of the vessel for a ways, as if it were conducting an angiogram. Next, a blood-thinning saliva is forced into the victim, so that the loot can be easily extracted. In a feat of complicated muscular choreography, the mosquito simultaneously sucks and spits. The average female mosquito can absorb three times her own weight in blood. She digests it in about three days and is then ready to sting again.

Among the mosquitoes most wanted in the Meadowlands is the *Culex pipiens,* a.k.a. the northern house mosquito, a brown-beaked, hairy antennaed, gray-bodied hood that hangs out in sewage and in waste-contaminated runoff. It has made its mark as the pollution-tolerant mosquito. The *Aedes triseriatus,* a.k.a. the tree-hole mosquito, is brownish black with silvery white scales and inhabits a few forested areas of the swamps. The dark brown malaria-carrying mosquitoes of the species *Anopheles* are not as common on the meadows in recent years but they are easily identifiable; their legs are so thin as to seem negligible, and when they land they execute a headstand so that they appear less like a mosquito than a syringe.

When mosquito extermination began on the Meadowlands, the *Aedes solicitan* was the most prevalent mosquito. Now the *solicitan* has been bumped to second place, replaced by *Culex pipiens,* which thrived in the pools of non–salt water that Smith inadvertently created when he diked out the brackish water of the marsh. The *solicitan* is still spoken of by mosquito commission personnel with begrudging respect, however. With its wide wings and banded beak, with its love of strong warm winds, it is the dive-bombing F-14 of mosquitoes. "I'll tell you," Soccio said, shaking his head in his old office chair. "*Solicitans,* they'll hit you hard. They'll give you a wicked bite. I don't care if it's day, storm, night. They're gonna light on you and they are gonna bite you. They're a pretty nasty mosquito." The *solicitan* is different from the house mosquito in that it lays its eggs on dry land that it knows instinctively will soon be covered by brackish water. Recently, a pond had been drained on the Kingsland Marsh in Lyndhurst while an office building had its supports repaired; large numbers of *Aedes solicitans* immediately took advantage of the situation, and when their eggs subsequently hatched, approximately eight days later, the resulting young *solicitans* immediately descended upon a softball game on a nearby field. "Some people called me up and they said, 'Hey we're getting killed down here,'" Soccio remembered. "They said, 'We're getting hit in the hot wind.' So I'm thinking, 'Jesus! This is impossible!' As it turned out, this was a classic case of water management."

One summer day Soccio sent me out to meet some mosquitoes firsthand. He arranged for me to spend some time with a mosquito inspector named Victor Deserio, who would do the introducing. Victor is one of several inspectors who cruise the environs of the Meadowlands performing mosquito reconnaissance and, when necessary, engaging in combat. Victor is forty-seven years old and of medium height with a wiry but muscular build that once served him well as an amateur boxer. On the day I hunted mosquitoes with him, he wore blue work pants and a blue T-shirt that featured an *Aedes solicitan* and the words "NEW JERSEY MOSQUITO CONTROL ASSOCIATION." Victor takes his job very seriously. He keeps his hair bristly short because one of the ways he performs mosquito reconaissance is by conducting landing counts, a procedure in which he allows mosquitoes to land on his body and then catches and counts them. Victor figures that long hair might make for miscounted mosquitoes. Victor's demeanor is intense and high strung, and when you are with him you get the feeling that if he were a mosquito he would be a hard-biting, wind-resistant *solicitan*—except that, as opposed to the *solicitan,* he abhors the meadows themselves. "There's something about that area that gives me the creeps," he says. "I mean, I'll go there. I go wherever there are mosquitoes. But I just don't like it."

I had heard of Victor from his colleagues before meeting him. The woman who dispatches mosquito control officers to areas within the commission's jurisdiction told me I would be meeting with a kind of a living legend. "Victor, he's the mosquito king," she said. "When people call with a mosquito problem and Victor's in their area, I say, 'Don't worry, you've got Victor.'" Victor is best known, though, as the inspector who has caught more mosquitoes in one outing than any other inspector on the commission, or, for that matter, anyone else the commission has ever heard about. His aptitude for successful mosquito capture perplexes people. As Soccio says,

"We don't really know why they go for him." I shook hands with Victor in front of the commission's garage, got in his truck, and headed out to see mosquitoes. We stopped briefly at a delicatessen, where I believe I gained some possible insight into his mosquito attraction prowess by watching him eat. He gulped down some coffee (sweet) and a big fried egg sandwich that was dripping with large quantities of ketchup and butter, his usual. Sure enough, in a few minutes, in a patch of woods that he decided to warm up in just down the road from the deli, Victor had mosquitoes landing all over him. "Basically," Victor said to me, "I'm very good at catching mosquitoes. It's just that regardless of the weather, I'm gonna catch 'em."

Touring mosquito-infested areas of New Jersey with Victor is like touring a red-light district with a vice squad detective. He described the mosquitoes' habits while simultaneously flushing them out into the open. The mosquitoes that initially were landing all over him were *Aedes triseriatus*. "They're a first-class pain in the ass," he said. "They bite pretty hard." As mosquito after mosquito made the mistake of setting down on Victor's arms or head or neck, he trapped them with a battery-powered hair dryer–shaped machine that sucked the insects into a screen-topped vial. He twisted and turned while pointing his machine at various points on his body as if he were performing an ancient martial art. "Now, a lot of the mosquitoes that will land on us this morning will be *triseriatus* and they are hard biters," he said. "You got *vexans* that are gonna land on us. You've got *ferrox* that are gonna land on us too. But anyway, the thing is you walk in and you get a *feel* for it. For instance, we'll walk in here, and I would say that within a couple of minutes, mosquitoes are gonna start landing on me. Sometimes, it's tough with sunlight because if they see me coming at them, they're gonna fly away and there's nothing you can do about that. After I'm done with this, what I'll do is I'll check that tire over there to see if it's got mosquito larvae in it. Tires are a major problem. They breed in tires. They love tires."

When I swatted my neck and noticed my own blood on my hand, Victor put the situation in perspective. "What that means is that he got you—well, *she* got you, I mean," he said. "She stuck her proboscis in you and got a blood meal. You see, basically, it's just like in life. In life, only the women will get you. They're the ones out for blood." (Victor is single.) When we examined Victor's catch his little tube was stuffed with frantic grayness. "Look at what I got here," he said. "We've got to have close to thirty here and I'm not even trying. See right there? See that one that just flew by? He's got a mask on his face? He's got the Pee-wee Herman eyes. That's a *ferrox.*" He held the tube up to my ear and I could hear the female mosquitoes' high-pitched wing beat tone, a kind of soft whine that is easily detected by the antennae of the males and which Victor too seems to easily detect.

The day was growing overcast, and we walked out of the woods and headed toward the Meadowlands despite Victor's misgivings. On the way, we sipped coffee and talked about the reputation that mosquito work has among the general public. "People say to me, how shitty is your life? You catch mosquitoes for a living," Victor said. "For a lot of people, it's just a summer job, they just pass through. But it's important to me. For example, it's important that I get a good landing count. That was an okay landing count back there. But I mean, at nine twenty-five on a sunny day, that was an *excellent* count. We now know that there's definitely a population there. I mean, you walk your dog in the woods there and you're gonna get hammered. That's important." I brought up his landing count record.

"Yes, I have the all-time greatest number," he said. "Which is a lot. One hundred and fifty-two at one time. That was a couple of years ago. They were flying all over and everybody was running out of the woods and I said, 'Screw this. I'm gonna get a landing count.' When I had the one hundred and fifty-two that day, I was just listening, like this . . ." He leaned back in the seat of his pickup and pressed his whining, mosquito-filled specimen tube to his ear. He said, "Everybody thought I was nuts." He added, "I guess in my mind I'm the fastest guy in the West."

Out in the Meadowlands, on a tide gate over Berry's Creek that was built into the side of the old mercury dump, we met Steve Pavel, a twenty-year veteran of the mosquito commission, who grew up in Lyndhurst and is comfortable with the area. As opposed to Victor, Steve was very laid-back; when we began talking, he lit up a cigarette and leaned out over the flat brown-green water as he smoked. Steve told me about the mosquitoes he deals with today on the meadows. He said *solicitans* can still be a problem. "We get 'em with moon tides," he said, "and they'll tear you apart. *Boom!* They stick to you like darts." East Rutherford's portion of the Meadowlands used to be infested, he said, until the Meadowlands Sports Complex was built there. Today, things are more routine. "I mostly dip and map," he said. "And then I call the helicopter and if there's a problem it sprays. Basically, I ID a lot of *Culex pipiens.*" While Steve and I spoke, Victor had darted off into the little pools of polluted water and continued to trap mosquitoes. Watching Victor, Steve commented on Victor's renown as a mosquito trapper. "I have a hard time getting them to land on me. I can be standing next to him while he's getting landing counts and I won't even get bit. I don't know why."

Just then, Victor interrupted to say that he had captured a

ferrox. "A *ferrox* mosquito is very hard to catch," Victor said. "They have that extra huge wingspan. You almost have to let them get you with their proboscis. But I don't actually let him bite me. I rarely get bit."

We all left the tide gate together and drove up to the mosquito commission's base camp in the Meadowlands, which is a little helicopter pad and a trailer on the north end of the North Arlington dump.

We took a detour down a dirt road that led to the shore of the Hackensack River and we got out of the truck to look across at Snake Hill. "You should have seen that place back when I was a kid," Steve said, pointing at the black cliff in the distance. "It was scary as hell, all these weirdos walking around at that asylum up there, and wrought-iron fences and criminals. In high school, we used to drive out there and then throw a guy out of the car and drive away and watch him panic. That place was really something."

Victor poked around halfheartedly looking for *Aedes solicitans,* and then urged us to move on. "I'm sorry," Victor said, "I still don't like this area one bit."

I got back in Victor's truck, which was so hot and humid that I cracked my window.

We stopped once more before our final destination at a polluted stream where Victor dipped and caught *Culex pipiens* larvae, and then to a field of dumped tires, where Victor again dipped and trapped. By this time, I got the feeling Victor was hoping to be the first person in northern Jersey to capture a disease-carrying Asian tiger mosquito—the latest dangerous breed to move into the state, having made its way to the southern region of the United States via water-filled tires— because when he returned without any he seemed disappointed. He did, however, have *triseriatus* larvae, which wriggled underwater like little Houdinis struggling to emerge from body bags, and he pointed out that a *solicitan* had landed on me and was strutting its white-banded back legs, preparing to extract a blood meal. "You know *solicitans* can carry encephalitis," he said, matter-of-factly. "That's why some people aren't crazy about taking landing counts."

At last, we drove slowly to the top of the landfill in North Arlington. We followed a dump truck up the hill. It was filled with trash, and it spilled discarded Bible literature into the breeze. The commission's helicopter pad and little trailer both looked north through a vista of abandoned dumps, polluted streams, and fields of bread-crust-colored reeds. Victor immediately jumped out of his truck and began a landing count. Steve lit another cigarette. He looked back at Victor and then turned to the skyline. He exhaled. "It's beautiful up here," Steve said. "We're one hundred and thirty feet up. You can see New York. A lot of times I watch the sunset up here. You should see it. Absolutely beautiful. You see a lot of pheasant. That over there is an old landfill. It's closed up. It was just regular garbage. Well, that's what they said they put in it. Who knows what was in the trucks? They're still dumping on the other side of this hill we're on, but when they were dumping garbage in this spot, it was hell. They were dumping down garbage on us. We had a jet helicopter. Stuff went right into the jets. It was a problem."

Steve turned around when he heard Victor shouting. "Hold on a minute!" Victor yelled. "Look at the size of *this* one!" Victor was watching his arm, his capture device at the ready; he seemed to be telepathically encouraging the mosquito to set down. When it did, Victor got in his truck and began taking notes.

Steve continued. "See," he said, "there's a piece of the George

Washington Bridge way up there. And over there that's the East Rutherford meadow. I think they might build on that." He lit another cigarette. "Rainfall is our killer down here," he said. "You get two inches of water and you're dead. And there's a lot of moon tides and that's a problem. And you're not gonna stop that. Basically, out here in the Meadowlands, there's always water somewhere. It's just control, that's all it is, and it's a lot of work. It's work all year long. Years ago, the signs on the trucks said mosquito extermination, but now they just say mosquito control. That's because it's a losing battle."

Suddenly, Victor was shouting again from inside his truck. "Holy shit! I think she got me!" he was saying. "*Look!* Look at how fat she is!" We ran over. Victor was pointing at a mosquito fat with blood in his landing count vial. "Holy shit, she did! She got me! Oh, I don't like that." He put down his clipboard and his specimen tube and stepped out of his truck. "No, I don't like that," he said. "Now, how did she get in here?" He looked at his specimen tube, which was correctly sealed shut, and then he noticed that the window on the passenger side of his truck was cracked. He looked at me. "*You* left your window open," he said. "You know, I don't let them get me. The window in my truck is never open."

I apologized profusely.

Victor collected himself. "I sat in the truck because I didn't want to get bit by *solicitans*," he said. "And then I think I hear one while I'm doing my paperwork and I think I'm losing it. Then, I get hit." He brushed his hair and shook his head as if he thought there might be another mosquito in the car—he couldn't be sure of anything now. He seemed shaken up. "Oh well," he said finally. "It's over and done with. I'm putting her ass in the refrigerator."

Steve drove back down the dump and Victor gave me a lift

back to the Mosquito Commission's headquarters. During the drive, I kept my window closed tight and I didn't mention what I had done and I began to think maybe Victor had forgotten about being stung, until we came to a stoplight and Victor started shaking his head again. "I'm sorry," he said. "I just can't believe it," he said. "I can't believe I got bit by a goddamn *solicitan*."

Treasure

SHORTLY AFTER WE HAD COMPLETED OUR FIRST EXPEDITION across the Meadowlands, when we were still sore and blistered and wondering if we could ever muster the energy for another one, my friend Dave faxed me a photograph from a local paper that showed an eighty-three-year-old man leisurely canoeing in the very place we had just struggled to explore. The man turned out to be Leo Koncher, a Kearny resident who has lived in the Meadowlands his entire life. Leo is five feet eight inches tall and has silky white hair and a slightly impish grin. He is a retired machinist and he typically dresses in shirtsleeves and khakis, as if he were in the middle of an unfinished project. He is a widower, and his home is a ramshackle field station stuffed with gear and equipment for the various expeditions he regularly undertakes into the Kearny Marsh, among other places in the Meadowlands. The first time I visited him there I introduced myself by telling

him of my interest in the Meadowlands, and he quickly
cleared off a couch, mentioning, as he often does, his late
wife. "My wife died ten years ago and the place is kind of a
mess," he said. Then, just as quickly, he got up from the
couch and took me on a tour of some of the things he carries
with him when he's out touring the marsh. He showed me
the marsh mud-walking equipment he had constructed by
securing an old shoe to the bottom of a big plastic bucket and
by then securing the bucket-shoe into a plastic milk crate.
"We are able to walk very nicely with these," he said. He
showed me the underwater observation devices he had made
using, in one case, the lid of a garbage can and a plastic sewer
pipe and, in another case, a longer sewer pipe connected to a
watertight flashlight. In addition to his gear, he showed me a
closet full of phosphorous rocks he'd collected in Franklin
Township, New Jersey—the rocks glow in the darkness in a
specially designed phosphorus rock display closet under his
front stairs—and a fiery landscape by Vincent van Gogh on
the wall of his living room. "It's probably a copy," Leo said,
shrugging off the painting. When we finished the tour and
Leo sat down, he put his hands on his knees and in his soft
calm voice said, "There's so much I have to tell you."

Leo Koncher was born in Harrison, New Jersey, the son of
Lithuanian immigrants. He worked as a machinist during
World War II and served in the Eighth Air Force in England,
where he repaired planes. As a boy, in his teens, he and his
friends would swim in the streams and creeks of the Meadowlands and sun themselves on the docks on the Hackensack
River. Like most children in those days, he crabbed on the
meadows in his spare time. The meadows were behind dikes in
Hudson County and a person could walk for miles where now
he or she must canoe. Sometimes Leo and his friends would

grab on to the back of the sand barges running down the Hackensack and into the cold black water of Newark Bay and hitch a ride down the Kill van Kull to Bayonne where they would steal brass portals off the old, rotting clipper ships. Once, at midnight under a full moon, in the middle of the bay, Leo and a friend were in a little sailboat that overturned and they had to hold on until morning when another boat came by and carried them back.

As an adult, Leo continued to make forays into the Meadowlands, but he began his most extensive explorations approximately twenty years ago when he bought a canoe at a garage sale. "The water looked inviting, so I went in, and I've been going in ever since," he said. Leo began exploring the meadows to an even greater extent after his wife died. In 1986, when Leo's son wrecked Leo's only car, Leo built a device that allows him to carry the canoe the mile or so down the hill from his home to the park on the Kearny Marsh. This device utilizes two bicycle wheels and a three-quarter-inch metal shaft that he specially designed for the task in his backyard workshop. The roof of his workshop is decorated with salvaged stumps of cedar trees from the old Meadowlands forest.

Leo has about him a determined restlessness, and depending on the weather, he canoes as many as three or four times a week. Heavy rain is the only thing that stops him from going out on the Kearny marshes. In the winter, when the water on the marsh freezes, he rides a bicycle on the ice and wears an innertube around his waist as a precaution against drowning. "You really don't need it because the bike makes a hole and the handlebar bridges the gap and you can pull yourself up and you have winter clothes on so it's like a wet suit," he said in his flat, matter-of-fact tone. "It's amazing. You're warm in about a minute." During his canoe trips, he has noticed certain peculiarities about the water in the Kearny Marsh: in the winter, for instance, the water that is most polluted is least likely to freeze. The day on the marsh that Leo talked about more than any other is the day that the water in the Kearny Marsh became suddenly clear. All of a sudden, Leo saw the bottom for the first and last time. He was amazed and he paddled around feverishly, seeing all that he previously had only imagined, as if it were a dream. "You could see great huge trees lying on their sides," he said. "Those were the trees in the cedar forest. I spent the whole day out there."

In the past few years, Leo has become an unofficial poet laureate of the Meadowlands. He has chronicled his trips on the marshes with frequent dispatches to the letters pages of local papers. He recently gave the Kearny Public Library a series of photos that he had taken at various times of the year from both his canoe and bicycle. The photos are of giant huckleberry bushes on the old dumps; the marsh in the early morning when a mist covers the lakes for as far as you can see; the marsh at sunset when the reddish outline of the reeds licks the gray sky like flames; the snow-white flowers of the marsh-mallows, and the phragmites in fall when they turn a dusty brown. The themes of his collected letters are the natural beauty of the marsh and the beauty of the creatures who live there, as told by a solitary wanderer. An example:

Dear Editor:

While canoeing in the Kearny marshes (a beautiful area that boasts about 50 lakes), I came across a sea gull. The Bird was tangled in a long red ribbon wound around a tree stump. It was soaked and bitten, but I finally cut the poor creature free. It swam away wobbly toward some other sea gulls, but they flew away. After about 15 minutes I wondered if the sea gull I had freed could still fly. Finally the liberated bird soared into the air, circled overhead and disappeared. What a heartwarming sight!

Leo F. Koncher,

Kearny

Leo is in astonishingly good health for an eighty-three-year-old. He tells people that paddling on the marshes saved his life. After he had heart surgery a few years ago, he couldn't walk more than a few blocks but he could paddle on the marshes for hours at a time, which he did as a kind of therapy. One time Leo took me out on an old railroad bridge forty feet over the Passaic River. Many of the railroad ties on the bridge were burnt out so that the path was like the smile of a man with no teeth. I was walking slowly in an effort to keep from falling in, and at several points we both had to get on our hands and knees to climb between faraway ties. I expressed concern. "What are you worried about?" he finally asked me. I said I was worried about falling into the river. Leo shook his head in bemused disgust. When we got to the end of the bridge, he had me look up to see the elevated span stuck straight in the air like a rusted knife. "It's beautiful, isn't it," he said. "This is really the best view." When we climbed back off the bridge and returned to his house, he showed me another letter he had written to a local paper, and after I read that letter his cavalier attitude made more sense.

Dear Editor:

Hundreds of sea gulls feed on the North Arlington dump. Some eat so much they can hardly fly and are easy prey for the hawks. Some sea gulls get tangled in debris and when this happens, the birds die a slow agonizing death. From time to time I was fortunate to spot some of these entangled sea gulls and save a few. I am convinced that it would be a blessing if when our time comes to go, it would be on the wings of a hawk. Oh, well, as Peter Pan said, "Death must be a wonderful adventure."

Leo F. Koncher,
Kearny

Leo Koncher is always searching for something when he goes out on expeditions into the swamp. One thing he searches for is a relic of one of the old plank roads that once crossed the Meadowlands. Specifically, he looks for remnants of the old road from Jersey City to Bellevlle. The Belleville Turnpike was built in 1765 by Colonel John Schuyler to carry copper from his mine. The road was macadamized in 1914, but some of the cedar planks were reported to be still around, long after cedar roads were out of fashion. Leo knows this and is bent on finding a piece of the old road. He occasionally puts in calls to state and local officials regarding the whereabouts of the planks. "It ought to be there," he often says, "and my question is, why hasn't anybody found a piece of it yet?"

Another thing Leo searches for is pirate treasure. Tales of pirates in the Meadowlands are numerous; pirates are the first instance of organized crime in the Meadowlands. The stories are all loosely based on the fact that in the 1700s, New York Harbor was filled with criminals. Pirates preyed on ships filled with the pelts and furs brought in by trappers in New Jersey and New York. Often the pirates were simply the crews of the pelt- and fur-carrying ships in mutiny against the ship's commander; for this reason, trading companies routinely sent twice as many men as necessary on voyages in expectation of a captain being forced to kill off a large percentage of his men. In the days that preceded jury tampering, the pirates found other ways to influence the courts. In 1701, at the trial of

Moses Butterworth, in New Jersey, a pirate said to be a member of the crew of Captain William Kidd and several of his associates broke in and took control of the courtroom. They were "armed to the teeth," according to one account, and they held the governor of New Jersey hostage for five days. The pirates would plunder boats in New York Harbor, race to the spit of land that separates the harbor and Newark Bay (and today is Bayonne), abandon their first boat, run over the wooded hill, jump in a second boat, and then flee north into the Meadowlands where they would disappear in the little creeks and forested streams. After a while, the pirates not only stole cargoes but the ships' money chests as well, and they kidnapped and raped women and children. "In the years following the Revolution, the criminal acts of these river and harbor pirates increased to so great an extent it became unsafe for small vessels to anchor anywhere in New York bay," wrote Daniel Van Winkle, the former Hudson County historian.

The story goes that eventually the pirates were tracked to a camp near an area called Point-No-Point, which was in the cedar forests on the neck of land that separates the Hackensack and Passaic Rivers as they empty into Newark Bay— land today occupied by truck farms, warehouses and a diner. Sheriffs in New York and New Jersey convened and gathered several hundred men, including what was then the entire male population of Jersey City and Bayonne. The men assembled boats, and naval officers were put in command of several flotillas. Just before daylight one morning they began their attack, sweeping up through Newark Bay. When the flotilla fired their howitzers, a large fleet of pirate boats fled up into the Meadowlands. Van Winkle wrote: "It was one of the most thrilling and bloody battles New York port has ever witnessed, and is only paralleled in degree by the earlier battles

with the Indians." The pirates who had not been killed or captured now headed deep into the swamps, into an area that was
thick with tall cattails and cedars, dark with sluggish water
and filled with black snakes, perhaps Berry's Creek.

The sheriffs waited until morning to strike. When the sun
came up, the ships fired their guns into the forest. Then a
group of eighteen heavily armed volunteers entered the creek
and rowed slowly into the swamp. An hour later, those waiting
at the mouth of the creek heard a long bout of gunfire, which
then ceased and was replaced by a preternatural calm. None of
the volunteers returned. After a while, the authorities decided
to burn the pirates out of the Meadowlands. It is said that this
fire burned the meadows from Point-No-Point all the way
north to Little Ferry, seven miles away. It burned for three days
and destroyed everything, including the cedar forest.

There was a time when historians went out of their way to
vouch for the accuracy of the story. "[T]he facts are as narrated
in old records, which are to be quoted as reliable and authentic," one historian wrote. I read another account in which the
author swore he himself had read firsthand accounts of the
pirate battle. And there are still other accounts that speak of
specific bands of brigands who hid in the woods along Belleville
Turnpike and plundered stagecoaches as they traveled from
Philadelphia to New York and that when the authorities burned
them out, they burned the last stand of old cedar forest. Today,
though, the pirate stories are considered to be apocryphal,
concocted by a generation that maybe felt guilty about having
cut down their forest.

Leo has heard all the old pirate stories and he has heard
they may be false, but he is convinced that the pirates and
brigands would have stashed or at least dropped some of their
loot near the edge of the old turnpike. He thinks the roots of

the old trees may hold gold coins. He uses his mud-walking gear to search for such coins. And he looks along the swampy bottom of the marsh with his underwater observation devices. "Of course, I don't know what you'd do if you found anything," he said. "The IRS would be all over you."

Sometimes, I get the feeling that Leo is searching for something else that he isn't really telling me about, such as the time when I was out in his canoe and out of the blue he recounted for me a story he had read in a magazine that concerned a man who thought his lost love came to him one day as he was waking in a hospital bed—he gave me a copy of the story and told me that it meant a lot to him. Most of the time, however, he announces a specific goal for a given canoe trip. One day I went out in Leo's canoe and we were specifically hunting for treasure. He sat in the middle on a kind of padded lawn chair. He was wearing his khakis, a long-sleeved white shirt, a red-and-white handkerchief around his neck to protect him from the sun, and a cap advertising Domino's Pizza. The bow on Leo's aluminum canoe said *Born Free*. Leo told me to sit in the back and paddle, although he became disappointed with my speed and eventually commandeered the paddle and did it himself. As Leo toured me through the marsh, he recalled canoeing in a swamp in Florida with his late wife. At one point on the trip, Leo apparently thought he was tying up their canoe to the roots of a mangrove tree but the roots turned out to be snakes. "My wife got hysterical," he said. He also told me about the hunters he occasionally meets during duck hunting season—"It can be a war zone out here," he said—and he took me to a little hunters' blind hidden away on an island of reeds. "Go ahead, pull up close," he said. "I want you to see this. You may find it rather unpleasant."

When I stood up in the canoe to look in, I saw thousands of flies. I looked back at Leo. He grinned.

Leo knows all the channels in the reeds in the Kearny Marsh intimately, so we crossed it with ease and pulled *Born Free* ashore next to a large fenced-in electrical transformer with danger signs posted along its fences. Leo carried a hoe that he planned to use to dig in a secret spot beneath the Belleville Turnpike—the pirates might have accidentally dropped some loot there when they were hiding alongside the old turnpike. As we made our way between a creek and the transformer, we came upon a man named Walter. Walter was heavyset and jocular and in his early sixties, and he was fishing from a folding chair along the banks just a few yards from his car.

"I'll tell you, Leo, you're nuts," Walter said by way of a greeting, as he rose from his chair and waved hello. He had a huge grin on his face. "Why don't you use the road like normal people, Leo?" Walter was shaking his head and smiling. He turned to me and continued. "You know, it's incredible," Walter said. "I see him all the time. I come out here in the winter, I see the tracks. It's him on his bicycle! I mean, he's incredible! Hey, by the way, Leo, I saw that toxic truck over there sitting in the water and leaking all that stuff. I thought you were going to take care of that, Leo. You know, Leo, I'm very disappointed in you." Walter grinned again.

Leo didn't say anything. He looked at me from under the bill of his Domino's Pizza cap and rolled his eyes. Then he said, "He's my friend. He's here every time I come out."

"You looking for treasure, Leo?" Walter asked.

"Yup," Leo said.

"Well, I'm just here fishing," Walter said.

I asked some questions about the fish he was catching—carp—and Walter began waxing sentimental about his fishing spot. "Hey, you know, a lot of us care about the area out here," he said. "I mean, it sure is interesting. Just look at all your birds." He had to shout as a tractor trailer passed by. "Boy, I love my cormorants and I *love* my kingfishers," he said. "And you should hear my brother. He can make the sound of one of those kingfishers that's unbelievable. It's incredible!"

Leo cut Walter short and motioned for me to follow him, which I did, and we left Walter behind. A quarter of a mile or so later, Leo finally stopped and pointed to a sandy patch of ground. He said, "The plank road would have been here, I figure." He scratched at the ground in a little hole filled with the broken pieces of phragmites and then turned to me with a look of shock on his face. "Someone's been here," he said. He continued scratching at the earth with his hoe in various places and then he reached down and picked up a small circular piece of metal. It wasn't gold but it appeared to be ancient. I was very excited, but Leo was blasé. "It's a button," he said. "It's probably very old. Here, you can have it." I insisted he keep it but he refused.

We dug a little more with no success and then we headed back for the canoe.

On the way, we passed Walter, who shouted out. "Hey, Leo!" he said. "Did you find anything?"

We showed him the button. "Look at *that*," Walter said. "Looks pretty old."

"It could be from the Revolutionary War," Leo said, matter-of-factly.

"It looks old, all right," Walter said.

At that moment, we all noticed the smell of a skunk, its dead body lying just a few feet from us on the side of the road in a grave of trash.

"Hey, Leo. I wonder if that was the same skunk I had in my

backyard," Walter said. "I wonder if it was the one that came out from my cemetery and crawled into my backyard. I live right next to the big cemetery up on the hill there, you know, Leo."

"My wife is buried in that cemetery," Leo said.

"Oh," Walter said.

Walter put his hands in his pockets and we all stood around not talking for a while. A car pulled up carrying four guys who spoke mostly Spanish. They asked us for directions to the Meadowlands Sports Complex, and Walter made hand signals to indicate the route they should take. Leo waved me on.

"Well, I'll see you later, Leo," Walter said, cheery again.

Leo canoed us back to the Kearny playground, and we put his canoe on my car and made our way up the hill to his house. I asked him if he expected to ever find any treasure. "Probably not," he said, "but what else are you going to do when you're retired?" We pulled down his little street and into a parking space two doors from his house. As I was about to drive away, Leo stopped me and said, "Do you see that house right there?"

I nodded.

"Well, there was a woman who lived there and she just died," he said. "Right after my wife died, she wanted me to move in with her. I don't know. Maybe I should have. She was kind of crazy, if you ask me. But maybe I should have taken her up on the offer. Anyway, when she finally died, they went in there and the place was crawling with cockroaches. She had been sick for a long time. There were just cockroaches everywhere. So they set off one of those bombs that's supposed to kill everything. Next thing you know, the guy next door has got roaches crawling all over his house. Now he's thinking about setting off one of those bombs in his house. I don't know what will happen then. I've never had any problems with roaches before in my place but if he sets off that bomb they'll probably come running over to *us*. Then I don't know what we'll do. I mean, maybe I'll have to set off a bomb too. I don't know." Leo began to walk away. "Oh well," he said. "Good-bye."

Digging

DIGGING IN THE MEADOWLANDS IS AN ODDS-ON PROPOSITION, as opposed to, say, prospecting for gold in Alaska or drilling for oil in the North Sea. In fact, most of the Meadowlands is underground. If, by magic or with the assistance of angels or with the help of a grant awarded through the Federal Enterprise Zone program, I could turn the bottom of the Meadowlands to the top and restore what was thrown into the muck back to its pristine predumped condition, the place would be instantly de-wasteland-ized. I'd sit on Snake Hill and watch as Swartwout's old muskrat-chewed dikes restored themselves and his farm returned and prospered and he danced in his fields with his family. I'd watch demolished buildings reassemble in the pristine marsh. I'd see barrels of toxic waste rise from the no-longer-polluted water and levitate harmlessly above the ground. Among the most enthusiastic of reanimated items from down under the Meadowlands would be the small bands of executionees, roaming together—their hands patting their chests, pinching their cheeks in wonderment—through the thick fields of wildflowers, each clumsy step rousing a pheasant or a wild turkey.

If a guidebook to the flora and fauna of the Meadowlands is ever written, it will have to include a chapter on bodies and their identification. There are no official statistics on the total number of human remains dumped there but stories of bodies being dumped in the meadows date back to the time of the Revolutionary War. One of the oldest stories tells of a prominent Newark citizen who disappeared and was at first presumed to have run away. His body was eventually recovered in the swamp after a keen-eyed Newark banker suspected foul play when he spotted the missing man's favorite British coin in the hands of another man who had subsequently taken up with the prominent citizen's young wife. A few years later, the body of a silversmith turned up in the meadows, a short while after a woman preparing a stew discovered one of the buttons from the silversmith's jacket in a bucket of muskrat entrails.

During Prohibition, when rumrunners were using its hidden creeks and streams as cover, the Meadowlands were especially popular as an execution site. In the summer of 1929, a bootlegger named Eugene Moran was taken for a ride in the Newark meadows, on the flats where Newark dumped its trash. A night watchman watched as two men drove a Packard down the road between the dumps. The two men jumped out and poured gasoline on the car. The Packard burst into flames. The two men ran to a getaway car—one of the two nearly falling. When the police and fire department arrived, they discovered that all the car's serial numbers had been chiseled away. Moran's identity was determined seven months later through dental records. Apparently, when the car began to burn, Moran had been lying unconscious on the backseat with a bullet through the back of his head. They never caught the two men who ran out of the dumps that night, just as they never caught all the people who dumped the bodies in the Meadowlands that were never found.

When I dig in the Meadowlands, I do so in an attempt to rouse some of these people, places, or things from their sleep in the swamp. There's plenty to dig for out there besides bodies. But when my friend Dave and I first started digging, a couple of summers back, it just seemed natural that we should dig first for the most notorious of all the people, places, and things buried in the Meadowlands, Jimmy Hoffa. We figured it was worth a shot.

If the Meadowlands were a nation, the Hoffa story would be its great national epic, a Mob-related Nibelungenlied, with poetic stanzas memorializing various dumps and the Giants end zone. The particulars of Jimmy Hoffa's burial in the Meadowlands are mostly derived from various oral histories recounted by people you wouldn't turn your back on for five minutes, much less trust for directions in a landfill, and for this reason there are a number of versions of the Hoffa story, some of which do not even mention the Jersey meadows at all. (In one scenario, Hoffa was driven not far from where he was last seen, to Central Sanitation Services, in Hamtramck, Michigan, and disposed of "by means of a shredder, compactor and/or incinerator . . . ," in the words of an FBI agent's affidavit. It should be mentioned, however, that FBI search dogs found no trace of Hoffa's scent at Central Sanitation Services.) All the most widely accepted versions of the Hoffa kidnapping story mention the Meadowlands, however. Most of them describe him as being buried in the Giants end zone, a theory that stems from the Teamsters' close association with some of the less-than-reputable people associated with some of the firms involved in the construction of the Meadowlands Sports Complex but a theory that I personally do not hold a lot of stock in. My favorite theory about the whereabouts of Jimmy Hoffa in the Meadowlands goes something like this:

James R. Hoffa, the former head of the United Brotherhood of Teamsters, disappeared on July 30, 1975, from the parking lot of the Machus Red Fox restaurant in Bloomfield Township, Michigan, a suburb of Detroit. At the time, the Mob was said to have been unhappy with Hoffa's attemps to regain control of the union after being released from jail in 1971 and wanted to see him out of the way. Hoffa was scheduled to meet with Anthony Giacalone, a.k.a. Tony Jack, in the parking lot at 1 P.M. that day. Hoffa drove to the restaurant in his 1974 Pontiac Grand Ville and waited. He telephoned his wife at 2:30, upset. "Where the hell is Tony Giacalone?" he asked. "I'm being stood up." That was the last his wife heard from him. It is conjectured that Hoffa was then picked up at approximately 2:45 in a maroon Mercury driven by Chuckie O'Brien, Hoffa's estranged foster son (O'Brien was married to a divorced beauty queen, and Hoffa, socially conservative to a fault, disapproved). Hoffa sat in the backseat, where he is thought to have been knocked unconscious, probably with the butt of a gun. According to a vision had by Hoffa's daughter, he sat slumped over. Her vision also indicated that Hoffa was wearing a brightly colored polo shirt, a detail she apparently had no way of knowing but which turned out to be true. The soon-to-be-slain former Teamsters boss was then brought to the airport where he was allegedly strangled by either Gabriel Briguglio or Thomas Andretta, possibly with piano wire (piano wire strangling seemed to be almost protocol in several murders related to the Hoffa case). Hoffa's body was flown or perhaps driven to New Jersey and dumped in the Meadowlands. Variations on the same theory suggest that after being strangled Hoffa was stuffed in a fifty-five-gallon drum, which was in turn loaded on the back of a truck and possibly driven by an unwitting Teamster—Hoffa, unpretentious and hardworking, was loved by the Teamsters' rank and file—to a dump in the Meadowlands.

Everyone suspected in the abduction had an alibi. Anthony "Tony Pro" Provenzano was a ruthless Teamster boss who controlled the trucking industry in the Meadowlands at the time. He was an elected official of his Teamsters local, but the elections were the kind in which his opponents had a habit of showing up dead or beaten to a pulp during the campaigns. Tony Pro reportedly had a "falling out" with Hoffa while the two served time together in prison, and one theory suggests that he was the gangster awarded a contract on Hoffa. Thomas Andretta, Tony Pro's trusted associate, testified that Tony Pro was playing Greek rummy at Local 560 in Union City. Tony Pro held a press conference on the lawn of his condominium in Florida when reporters started asking him if he had anything to do with Hoffa's disappearance. "You guys make me look like a mobster. I'm not. I'm just a truck driver," he cheerfully told reporters, his tan belly hanging over his bathing suit. (*People* magazine published photographs of the interior of this particular truck driver's home that featured numerous concrete cherubs and an oil painting of his mother that he decorated daily with fresh-cut flowers.) As for Chuckie O'Brien, the FBI found blood in the backseat of the maroon Mercury he was driving that day, and no one could confirm his alibi—that he was playing cards at the Southfield Athletic Club with Tony Jack. But O'Brien later explained the discrepancy by claiming that he had been delivering a coho salmon to a judge and blood from the salmon had spilled all over the backseat of the car; by the time he delivered the salmon and had the maroon 1975 Mercury cleaned at a car wash, he had missed his scheduled card game. The manager of the car wash told the FBI that he hadn't seen any 1975 maroon Mercurys that day. A week later the car wash manager, who was forty-five years old, died of natural causes.

Despite all the alibis, the particular dump in the Meadowlands that was often cited remained a likely burial site for investigators, especially since the bodies of other mobsters who had reportedly been dumped there had also never been recovered. The suspected dump was the PJP landfill, a.k.a. Brother Muscato's dump. Brother Muscato's dump is a one-time salt marsh on the bottom of a hill in the Marion section of Jersey City. It sits across from an old power plant on a stretch of the Hackensack River known as Marion Reach. (The land was condemned in the 1930s as part of the construction of the Pulaski Skyway, the elevated highway that passes over the southern end of the Meadowlands.) A fireworks warehouse stood there until 1935, when it caught fire and exploded. In 1969, the marsh officially became a dump and was christened the PJP Sanitary Landfill. Two hundred truckloads of waste were dumped every day, much of it in barrels. Core samples taken later revealed a greatest hits list of toxins, including naphthalene, phenanthrene, methylene chloride, toluene, and ethylbenzene. The air around the dump soon acquired one of the worst reputations in the Meadowlands. A Jersey City official once said to me, "It had the most disgusting smells you could possibly think of." On July 8, 1970, the dump caught fire and most of its eighty-seven acres burned for fifteen years. The state closed it in 1974, but huge clouds of foul-smelling black smoke continued to waft out from the dump, sometimes impairing the vision of drivers on the Skyway, and an underground river of leachate threatened to erode the Skyway's support structure. The smoke blew into the nearby housing complexes. The Jersey City fire chief would not send his men into the dump, fearing for their safety. "Nobody knows for sure *what's* in there," he told a reporter. The fire was finally extinguished at the end of the eighties by Boots & Coots, a Texas firm that later was contracted to extinguish out-of-control oil rig fires after the war in the Persian Gulf. Up until the fire was put out, drivers and nearby Jersey City residents called the area "The Gates of Hell."

Despite PJP's reputation, Dave and I were eager to attempt to dig because this dump—in contrast to other possible burial sites mentioned in the months after Hoffa's disappearance—had never really been explored. In Waterford Township, Michigan, people who hoped to find Hoffa's body and collect the $275,000 reward dug with garden tools in a rattlesnake-infested field a few yards away from law enforcement officials' backhoes. The papers described a "picnic-like atmosphere" that included beer and soda. At the PJP landfill, on the other hand, the FBI got a warrant to dig through the dump in December of the year Hoffa disappeared, and then had their warrant extended, but instead of digging the agents just sat and watched the snow-covered site for several days. The FBI eventually asked the state police if they would be willing to dig, reportedly neglecting to mention to their law enforcement brethren the possibility that the dump contained poisonous gases capable of exploding, but the state police declined. The local Teamsters organization volunteered men for the job, and offered a ten-thousand-dollar reward of their own for their missing leader's body, but the FBI insisted that their agents be on hand when the Teamsters dug, and they never agreed on a mutually convenient date. When I went over to the Teamsters office to ask whatever happened with the dig, I got on the elevator that rode up the elevator shaft that Tony Pro was once allegedly thrown down (he said he just tripped). The elevator operator offered me a little tour of the building, and when I asked him about Hoffa said, "He was just here." My jaw must have been hanging open because the elevator operator was staring at me, until I realized the elevator operator was talking about Hoffa's son, Jimmy Hoffa, Jr., who was running for the presidency of the Teamsters union at the time. I was so shaken that I sat out in front of the building for a couple of minutes trying to calm down. In my unmarked car, I looked like an FBI agent with too much coffee in his system.

The morning that Dave and I set out to dig for Jimmy Hoffa was beautiful and sunny, and as we drove through Jersey City, we got lost and circled underneath the Pulaski Skyway a couple of times and wondered for a brief moment if a van full of Korean churchgoers might be following us. Initially, we could find no route into the area; the dump was surrounded by a highway, warehouses, and the river. The closest we could get to it was on the grounds of a driving range, where we rented a club and bought a bucket of balls and Dave hit out toward a reeded, grass-covered hilly area that I assumed was part of the dump in question. We were back in the car on a dead-end street that seemed to be just south of our goal, when we ran into a retired Jersey City fireman, who called himself Big John. Big John was trapping blue crabs off the old Hackensack River pier. We asked him if he'd ever heard of the PJP landfill.

"Are you kidding?" he asked us back. "I knew 'em all. PJP. Let's see Philip, John, and Paul—Philip Muscato, John Hanley, Paul Cappola—they're all my friends. Real nice people. But you know, it was garbage as far back as I can remember and I'm sixty-two years old. When I was a kid it was garbage, all garbage. We used to play underneath the Skyway and it was like a mountain, that's how high it was. And by the time I was thirteen, you could stand on top and touch the bottom of the Skyway. Then we used to go in there when I was a fireman. Actually, it might still be burning somewhere down there, to the best of my knowledge."

The crabs that Big John was catching were big and their claws were snapping as they sat in buckets in the back of his big car. Big John said, "Right now, they're mating so they don't feel like crawling in the traps, but when they're not mating I usually go home with about a dozen."

We asked how they tasted.

"They're fine," he said. "At one time, there used to be black oil on top of the water and the crabs would come out covered with oil. We called 'em tar babies. We'd boil them in water and they were damn good. But you know, now, people see a little puff of smoke and they say it's pollution and they're gonna die. I say, 'You don't wanna die? Hey, then go kill yourself!' "

Standing next to Big John was a guy named Mark, whose two sons were climbing out on an old crane that was once used to lift boats out of the river. "I moved from here out to Pennsylvania and now I have to move back," Mark said. "It's like you get cabin fever all year round out there. It's not like it is here. Here, you step in some place and you bullshit. Like this. That's why I bring my kids back to the city." At this, he stopped and looked at Big John's coffee. "Hey, how come you didn't get me any coffee?"

"Hey, look," Big John said. "Why don't you go down to the end of the street and wait for your brain to be delivered? It's due."

"Oh, you got *your* coffee," Mark said. He cracked a smile. "But nothin' for me."

"Hey," Big John said. "They got a street named for you. It's called One Way. *Get outta here!*" Big John motioned to Mark's two boys. "Hey, look at your kids," Big John said. He then pointed at the greenish brown water racing past. "Look. They're gonna go in the river, and if they go in, I ain't gonna go get 'em. Not me."

"They're used to Pennsylvania, climbing in all the trees and everything. No big deal."

"Oh, so I'm overprotective, is what you're saying?" Big John said. "Oh yeah, you know everything. You're a genius. Hey, you know, you could donate your brains to science. I mean, they're in perfect condition. They've never been used."

Mark relented. "Come on," he said to his kids. "Get down from there."

"Hey! *Hey!*" Big John said. "Don't start yelling at your kids. Be patient, for chrissake."

We followed Big John's directions and drove through the huge yard of a trucking firm. In a garage, we found a very serious-looking man with silver hair and a silver mustache who was surrounded by what seemed like a hundred people talking to him all at once. The man spoke Spanish. Dave translated for me as I asked the man who seemed to be in charge for permission to drive to the back end of the trucking yard and look for a way into the adjacent dump. (We felt it was best not to mention Jimmy Hoffa, given the difficult translation issues it presented.) The man nodded his head, and then everyone began talking to him again, and we drove on rutted swampy ground and eventually up little hills made of what looked like shredded roofing. We came to a fence and, beneath it, a moat filled with black scum-covered leachate. We had no canoe that day so we climbed up on top of our car to get a better view. There was no way in. Dave looked out across the landfill with his binoculars. He said, "Look! A shopping cart!"

A couple of weeks later, I contacted the New Jersey Department of Environmental Protection and made arrangements to take a tour of the PJP landfill site with Jeanette Abels, the operations manager of the remediation program that the PJP landfill is undergoing. I met her in a pullout along the highway, where there was a padlocked gate in the long fence. I jumped into her light blue Dodge Ram and signed a form stating that I wouldn't hold the state Department of Environmental Protection responsible if I was injured on or by the landfill. "We just had the grass mowed," said Abels as we drove in. She is a chemist by training and before her work in landfill remediation, she tested the shelf life of pharmaceutical products, such as treatments for head lice. She has short dark brown hair and a dry sense of humor—on her desk in Trenton she keeps a cartoon that features several flies watching a film entitled *Dumps of the World*—and her voice had a trace of her South Bronx childhood. "The state planted this grass," she said as we drove out into a big empty short-grass field along the Hackensack River. "It's our own formulation. It's what we call landfill fescue."

Injury seemed unlikely on the morning I was there. The old dump had been capped with clay, sand, and soil; the vents of a gas ventilation system dotted the surface of the rolling hill like periscopes. I might have felt differently had I visited a few years before, when PJP had been on fire. "When it was burning, this was Dante's *Inferno* out here," Abels said. "There were flames everywhere and it was like Yellowstone with geysers of steam and smoke. I think you can name any chemical and it was here. They took out thousands of drums and those were just the ones

151

that weren't consumed or spilled." Now, though, the PJP landfill is practically bucolic: a field of grass rolls down to the river, with woodland separating it from the road. "People say, 'Ah, you take care of that ugly thing in there.' But I say, 'Actually, it's one of the nicest spots around.' Of course, you do have to watch out for packs of wild dogs." Dave and I would not have been welcome on her landfill had we just wandered in; Abels routinely kicks people off. "Once I saw two guys walking out here," she said, "and they were wearing suits. And I said, 'Uhm, *what* do you think you're doing out here?' And one of the guys said, 'Well, you may think this sounds really silly, but I have a dream to build a church out here, under a bridge like this.' And I said, 'Okay, but you really have to leave,' which they did. They were very polite."

Abels walked me down to where the old dump's leachate stream flowed into the river—the state has yet to take care of that. As we walked, we put up a ring-necked pheasant: it said, "*Kuk-kuk!*" as if it were a shotgun being cocked. I decided not to bring up digging for the body of Hoffa at this point— it seemed impolite, given Abel's hospitality and the number of phone calls I had to make and the forms I had to sign just to take a walk on the PJP landfill. Besides, I felt certain that Hoffa was somewhere in this dump, and to dig him up would have done a disservice to his legend and to the myth of the Meadowlands. It would have been like finding out the name of the Unknown Soldier. Consequently, I was giving up the idea of ever digging for Hoffa at all, and I was instead looking for a sign that might tell that what was left of him really was in PJP.

Just then, at the bottom of the landfill, at a spot where the damp breeze blew up off the steely green river and into our faces, I looked down at my feet and saw a splotch of red in the freshly cut fescue. The red was part of a little lichen. The lichen grew in drab green stalks, each blotched with red. This particular lichen, I later learned, is known as British soldier, its color reminiscent of the red coats British soldiers once wore, and it grows on the moist ground of other old dumps in the Meadowlands. But kneeling there, on top of Brother Muscato's, above Jimmy Hoffa's reputed grave and above the reputed graves of scores of less well known others, I couldn't get over how much the lichen looked like a bloodied, amputated limb.

Dave and I didn't let our failure to dig up Jimmy Hoffa get in the way of further digging in the Meadowlands. We continued to hike through the dumps, on unmarked, reed-hidden trails, through jittery groves of garbage-supported aspen. In time, we became practiced Meadowlands excavationists and even developed a set of guidelines to be used when digging there. For example, it is wise to remember that normal metal detector usage rules do not apply in the Meadowlands. We learned this through experimentation. Initially, we went to old landfills, turned on our metal detectors, and, as is generally the practice, dug when the detector chirped excitedly. Unfortunately, given the refuse-rich nature of the local soil, the metal detectors almost always sounded. Dave found he was as likely to dig up a piece of metal—an old metal cable, an ancient screwdriver, a piece of steel wire–reinforced glass—at a spot suggested by a metal detector as he was at a site selected at random. With this in mind, we roamed the landfills, attacking with pickax and shovels the ground where the metal detector *didn't* signal. In Kearny, we dug at the site where old aerial photographs indicated rubble from London might have been dumped at the beginning of World War II, and we discovered lots of things that once possibly might have belonged to the city of London:

The middle of a broken brown brick, gasping out a fragment of its
maker's name: "DIALIT . . ."

The stone top of the step to an old building, cracked to bits but still
white

A big whitish brick, shouting its last words so loudly it seemed more
likely to be American: "FARNLEYI . . . NEARLE . . ."

A piece of sand-colored piping marked with the day's only complete
word: "SWANK"

A piece of something thick and dark gray and cylindrical that didn't
seem like metal but the metal detector went crazy when near it
and which I put in my basement until I started wondering about it
(I thought maybe it was radioactive or something) and moved it to
a spot out behind my garage.

That day, as we dug, a British Airways jet swooped out from the
clouds over us on its way to Newark as if it were an anxious bird
protecting her nest. After honing our skills in the London
Hills, we were eventually able to undertake what would be our
greatest semiarchaeological feat. We began our search for the
great neo-Roman train station that was ripped from its eight-
acre home on Eighth Avenue in New York City in 1964 to make
way for a new station and a sports and entertainment complex.
We began our search for New York's Pennsylvania Station. Not
the new Penn Station, which is modern and low ceilinged and
kind of like the lobby of an office building and still there
underneath Thirty-fourth Street, but the old Penn Station, the
one that was torn down and dumped in the Meadowlands.

Penn Station is difficult to find in the swamp, but it was
easy to spot when it was still in New York. Eighty-four thirty-
five-ton columns decorated its exterior, each constructed precisely as they had been in Rome, in four-foot-tall chunks,
connected with pegs. The station's interior was modeled after

the Baths of Caracalla, which was built in Rome between A.D. 211 and 217. The Roman version of Penn Station consisted of twenty-eight acres of dressing rooms, exercise rooms, libraries, gardens, and several cavernous halls filled with enough cold, hot, or lukewarm water to accommodate sixteen hundred bathers. (When considering Penn Station's design, Charles F. McKim of McKim, Mead and White, the architectural firm that designed the station, gathered a gang of workmen in Caracalla's ruins to see how it looked with humans.) Of the New York version of the Baths of Caracalla, an architectural critic wrote: "Through the careful manipulation of space and historic reference, Pennsylvania Station was made the gate to a great Metropolis." At nine-thirty on the night of November 26, 1910, the night Penn Station opened for use, two thousand people lined up on Seventh Avenue in hopes of walking through.

When Penn Station was torn down, architects like I. M. Pei and Philip Johnson and prominent New Yorkers such as Jacqueline Kennedy Onassis picketed in protest. An editorial in *The Times* lamented, "[W]e will probably be judged not by the monuments we build but by those we have destroyed." The protests marked the beginning of the modern historic preservation movement. But while it was a big deal when the station was torn down, it wasn't such a big deal when it was dumped. For a long time, my only clue to its post–New York whereabouts was an old undated newspaper photograph, in which the pillars appeared abandoned and sad. Then, I found an old newspaper story. "PENN STATION COLUMNS DUMPED IN JERSEY," the headline read. "DORIC SPLENDOR HAD AN IGNOBLE ENDING IN THE MEADOWS." The report was sketchy on details but it claimed that passengers on the Pennsylvania Railroad could see the old pillars from the train just before it ducked into the tunnel that crosses under the Hudson River. In the photograph accompanying the dispatch from the meadows, the huge granite columns that once guarded the station's perimeter were now scattered across an open field and disassembled into their prenatal four-foot chunks.

The article listed an address where the pillars were being dumped at the time—2800 Secaucus Road—so I set out for Secaucus on a winter morning to have a look. I stopped first at the Secaucus library, where the librarians didn't seem to believe me when I said that Penn Station had been buried on the Secaucus meadows until I showed them the old newspaper clipping. I searched through old Secaucus papers but found no more clues. (In retrospect, only something *not* dumped in the Meadowlands would have been news in Secaucus in those days.) I was traveling by foot so I took a cab to the address listed in the paper. The cabdriver had never heard of the construction firm mentioned in my newspaper clip, but he told me a story about his great-grandfather, who had once put on Shakespearean plays in Jersey City and acted the lead part himself and was always booed off the stage. On a lonely stretch of Secaucus Road, where 2800 should have been but wasn't, he let me out. On one side of me was a huge field of reeds cut by Penhorn Creek, and on the other was a truck yard the size of a village. I walked into the security office at the trucking yard where the guard was able to reminisce fluently about the smells of a slaughterhouse that was once nearby but was unable to offer any additional information about the whereabouts of Penn Station's remains. I began the long walk back to downtown Secaucus. Big rocks decorated the edge of the trucking company's property, and as I approached each one, I wondered if it might be one of the missing digits of the station. I was about to climb a fence and wander around the phragmites field when I ran into Al McClure, a Secaucus animal control officer, a friendly gray-haired man in his sixties who didn't know anything about Penn Station either but offered me a ride back to town. When he dropped me off, he only told me what I already knew. "I tell you one thing," he said. "If you dig out here, you sure as heck are going to find something."

I spent the next few weeks using computer telephone listing software and old phone books in attempts to contact former officials of the defunct demolition firms reputed to be involved in the station's burial. I spoke to a woman who didn't know what Penn Station was and couldn't talk anyway because she had to run out to a birthday party, to an attorney in New York City who knew a woman in college who he thought was related to the people who conducted the demolition and who had moved out of state, and to several uninterested answering machines. Eventually, I tracked down the Pennsylvania Railroad's chief engineer at the time. His name is Harry J. McNally, and he is retired and living in Florida. He remembered that a few of the eagles that decorated the building's facade were moved to other railroad stations—one in downtown Philadelphia, and another to one of the stations of the Long Island Railroad—and that people all over the country clamored for pieces of the station. (I read later the senior class of the high school in El Cajon, California, wanted to present one of the five-foot-tall, fifty-seven-hundred-pound eagles to the school as a class gift because El Cajon's athletic teams were nicknamed the Eagles.) McNally remembered that people followed the trucks out to New Jersey. But like everyone else I had spoken with he couldn't remember exactly where the pieces were dumped. When I asked him what else he could tell me about the old Penn Station, he said wistfully, "Oh, there are a million things," but did not elaborate.

As winter passed and spring came and the birds began nesting on the dumps again in the Meadowlands, I became convinced I would learn where Dave and I could dig for Penn Station. I had narrowed our site possibilities down to a field on the edge of a relatively modern plaza of office buildings built out over an old marsh, but I was still looking for a more decisive clue. It was then that Tony Malanka, the Secaucus dump owner I know, took me on a drive over to the house of Paul Amico, the former mayor of Secaucus. All the way over Malanka kept saying that if Amico, who had been mayor for thirty years, didn't know where Penn Station was, nobody would. We drove up into the high ground that is the center of the island of Secaucus, and when we arrived at his house, former mayor Amico shook hands with me and handed me his card, which read, PAUL AMICO, RETIRED MAYOR OF SECAUCUS. We sat down for tea in his kitchen. The subject of our chat turned to demolished buildings in the area. He mentioned that a diner he had once owned had been built on the disinterred remains of the New York City neighborhood that once stood off Times Square, where the Port Authority Bus Terminal is now. As for Penn Station, Retired Mayor Amico had only a vague recollection of its burial, so we passed the rest of the afternoon reminiscing about Secaucus's reputation as a place for pigs and trash. As mayor, Amico had hoped to implement a public relations program that would have deemphasized Secaucus's waste-related past and emphasized its long-forgotten relationship with flowers. "You know, Secaucus is well known for pigs and such, but before that we had fields and fields of flowers, all kinds of nurseries," he said. "There were flowers everywhere. Flowers, flowers, flowers. There were beautiful flowers. But we never got any credit for that. When I was mayor, I wanted to set up a little exhibit in town—you know, dedicated to flowers and the role that flowers had in Secaucus. Because, after all, why shouldn't we be known for flowers, really? Unfortunately, that never happened."

Finally, one hot day in September, I picked Dave up and we drove to a field in Secaucus and began to dig. It was the field that I was pretty certain was in the old *Times* photo; there was some construction going on in it so I thought no one would mind if we dug a little. In an attempt to triangulate the position of *The Times* photographer who photographed the displaced columns in 1964, using the tracks, a train signal, and some buildings in the distance, Dave climbed to the railroad track, which crosses the marshes and old dumps of Secaucus. Irritated trains honked at him indignantly. Next, we poked around in a large phragmites field, where we found hidden piles of rubble, none of them resembling Penn Station. We found a huge white rectangular stone of something—Dave worked for fifteen minutes to chip a piece off it—but we didn't have any idea of what it was. Soon we moved on to a bigger field where, as luck would have it, a backhoe had already been digging the week before, apparently in connection with the construction of a new office building. The ground was soft and easy to shovel. In just a few minutes, we dug up some old china, a few oyster shells, and a piece of glass that was Milk of Magnesia bottle blue. I suggested that we were digging through the grounds of a onetime pig farm, where restaurant garbage was regularly dumped, and Dave confirmed my hypothesis when he took a break and wandered off into an abandoned pig farmer's house that was hidden alongside Penhorn Creek in some reeds and trees. When I found him, he was up in the old pig farmhouse, and he shouted for me to come up, but I waited for him outside. The place was falling apart, and there was no way I was going in there.

From that point on, we began uncovering larger pieces of rock, and soon everything started looking as if it might possibly be from Penn Station. We pulled up several bricks imprinted with the dates 1912–1913, and we found a piece of marble. When we came upon any kind of big rock, we were convinced it was going to be a column or an eagle. But after a couple of hours, and with no decisive article, we quit for the day and drove into downtown Secaucus where we had beer and sandwiches at the Stadium Restaurant. No one asked us why we were covered with dirt or why there were shovels sticking out of the back of our car. When we had finished lunch and were about to pay the bill, the waitress convinced us we had to try the coffee. "It's incredible coffee," she said. "I don't know what they do to it. I think it's the water."

All through lunch Dave had been disappointed that we had not made a major find, but when we drove past the field at the end of the day, we stopped the car and he looked at the old pictures again and puffed his cigar and then said, "It's got to be out there." I felt the same way, and the next day I drove around the area some more, feeling as if I was closer to finding Penn Station than ever before. In the morning, I met the operator of the backhoe that was coincidentally working in the area. He was pulling up more of the same kinds of things that we had been finding: unexplainably interesting hunks of stone. I asked him if he'd seen Penn Station in the course of his excavations, and he said he'd pulled up a couple of huge pieces of concrete and steel and wondered about them. I told him I would be interested in seeing these items. "Jeeze, I forget where I put 'em now," he said. I managed to find the pieces he was talking about back by the abandoned pig farmer's house. After photographing them, I went back to the backhoe operator and gave him my card. "Call me if you find anything," I said.

Digging

I was driving away from the dig site when I spotted a man in his late thirties working in the yard of a welding business, which was across the street from a go-go bar that was once called Tammany Hall. (Back then, it was owned by the Krajewskis, a famous Secaucus pig farming family, one of whom, Henry, ran for president a number of times in the forties and fifties, campaigning in a white Cadillac under the slogan NO PIGGIE DEALS.) On a whim, I pulled over and asked the man if he'd seen any big old pillars around. To my surprise, he remembered having seen some just down the street on a nearby trucking firm's property when he was a kid. I sprinted to my car. I had previously been warned away from the grounds of this particular trucking yard by security guards, but I looked at my maps again and calculated a path past the security booth that seemed to be on a small public street. I drove in slowly, flashing the skeptical-looking guard a confident matter-of-fact wave. In a few seconds, I entered a huge lot filled with dozens of tractor trailer trucks, their drivers either asleep with their feet on the steering wheels or milling around in small crowds. They eyed me curiously. I was nervous, but in the corner of my eye, behind an aluminum-covered lunch truck, only a few hundred yards up Penhorn Creek from where Dave and I had dug for hours the day before, I saw three huge chunks of rock surrounded by minimal dirt and debris. I parked the car and electric-locked the doors and ran over to touch them and I knew in an instant what they were.

It is difficult to describe exactly how I felt at the moment I found my pieces of Penn Station, with the cold granite of the column beneath my hand. I thrust my clenched fist into the air, relishing the fact that I had laid hands on a piece of re-ruined Rome that might one day be dug up by an archaeologist who could then quite possibly mistake the Meadowlands for a large and major transportation hub or the center of a great city, before eventually realizing it was just a big dump. I collected myself and saw that the rocks were definitely granite—pinkish dotted with black and gray—and that they were cylindrical in shape and roughly four feet long. In the bottom of each were several small holes, where joiners would have allowed one to be stacked upon the other, à la the classic Roman column. They were immovable due to their tremendous weight. I chipped off several pieces of one column with great difficulty. (Only later would I come back with a chisel and, with Dave's assistance, successfully break off a good-sized chunk to take home with me.) I shot two rolls of film of the columns. I began to attract the attention of several truck drivers, and then a Barbadian truck driver offered to take pictures of me standing next to it. I accepted. One of the truck drivers had begun using his index finger to draw imaginary circles adjacent to his temple. The eastern European woman behind the counter of the lunch truck asked me if I was a professor.

I left with the bits of chopped-up pillars and drove to a pay phone and called Dave to give him the news. Sometime later, I was able to get in touch with my wife, who was happy for me. In the afternoon, when my photos were developed, I drove to the nearest notary public and asked her to verify the date of my find—during lunch, I had become obsessed with the idea that someone else was going to attempt to find the remains of Penn Station and so I wanted proof that I had been there first. The notary stamped her name, Aida G. Zakhary, and the date, September 17, 1996, on my photos, and then she politely asked me what it was that I was standing next to in the photos she had just notarized. I told her about Penn

Station being dumped in the Meadowlands, but she had never heard of Penn Station. So I said it was the ruins of a great building that once stood proudly in New York City. She smiled and squinted a little and looked in my eyes and said, "Oh."

Bodies

IN THE SOUTHERNMOST PORTION OF THE MEADOWLANDS, ON a spit of land that is squeezed to a point by the Hackensack and Passaic Rivers as they reach their confluence in the roiled waters of Newark Bay, there are scores of old buildings and shells of buildings and ancient pieces of so many other structures large and small that the area itself can sometimes seem like a rotting corpse. You need an expert to identify the body. The person I have called upon to do so on many occasions is a retired detective from Kearny by the name of John Watson, who also happens to have more experience finding actual bodies in the Meadowlands than anyone I know. Watson stands five feet eight inches tall and weighs about two hundred pounds; he is sixty-two years old and mostly bald, but his arms and his chest are still bulky and strong and I often find myself happy that I am his friend: he's a nice guy, but you can tell he was a tough cop.

Watson began patrolling the Meadowlands in 1956, when

they were still mostly meadows. He was made a detective in 1980, he retired in 1985 and he was called back from retirement to testify in a murder trial that he doesn't really like to talk about. He does like to talk about what the area was like before so many of its businesses closed, in the time when a greater number of truckers and assorted underworld figures made the Meadowlands their home. "They called me 'The Shooter,'" he told me once, "'cause I'd shoot into the air once in a while. But the thing was, you had to let them know you meant business." He tells a story about the time he stood nose-to-nose with a big ornery truck driver in the middle of a trucking yard known to be particularly unruly. "The guy turns around to look at me, and right then I can kind of feel all the truckers kind of clearing back out of the room, giving us some space," Watson said. "So I've got my leather coat on and when he turns around, I push back the coat, the way we do so's I can get to the handle of my gun, and I say, 'Come on. Let's go.' And then I wait. And I'm staring at the guy and he's staring at me and everybody's watching us and I say, 'Look. I can't be wasting any more time.' So finally I see his Adam's apple just drop, just a little, and I remember at that point I knew I had him. So I said, 'Come on. Let's go.' And then I grabbed him and brought him down to the desk sergeant. That's how it went down there. It was like the Wild West."

Watson has a voracious appetite for all facts pertaining to the Meadowlands, facts that he is always willing to share. He particularly enjoys engineering books that speak to the one-time prowess of the Meadowlands' various bridges and buildings. When his wife, who is German, hosts relatives from overseas, Watson routinely drives them all down to south Kearny, where they are mesmerized by his tour of old industrial objects, and where they are able to identify particular bridges by name—Watson is convinced that Europeans appreciate the Meadowlands more than Americans, though he's not certain why. One fall afternoon, when the sky was clear and the air was crisp enough to make the little smoke puffs that rose out the smokestacks seem like healthy new-born cumulus clouds, I called him on the spur of the moment to take advantage of his Meadowlands knowledge. First, he said that he was too busy mopping his kitchen floor, but then he changed his mind and called me back, which startled me because I never left him my phone number—he had traced my call. "You know what?" he barked into the phone. "Come on down. I've gotta go out but I'll be right back. I have a lit-tle yard. It's kind of chintzy but you can wait there for me. Just so you know, my neighbors got two dogs, but they prob-ably won't bother you. Yeah, one's a poodle, and the other one's a pit bull."

I waited on his stoop.

When Watson pulled into a parking space in front of his house to pick me up, he was wearing a bolo fastened with a silver ram's head, dark blue corduroy pants, and a plaid shirt, which was long-sleeved, so you couldn't see the thick white scar on his arm that he got on the night he pulled a dead jazz saxo-phonist out of the Passaic River. (The saxophonist had just returned from Europe and couldn't find work so jumped off the old Lincoln Highway bridge.) Watson ran into the house, carefully tiptoeing across his kitchen floor, still wet in patches, and grabbed two nonalcoholic beers. He guzzled his down and I nursed mine in the car as we drove down the slopes of Kearny. As soon as he put the car in drive, he was in his tour guide mode. ". . . Now, according to the *Encyclopedia Ameri-cana*," he said, "not *Britannica*, now, but *Americana*—this area was settled first by Germans in 1752. And that's true." In a few minutes, we had reached the low flat area of the meadows. We passed the Kearny Marsh on the right and Mount Arlington, with its high tattered fringe of fresh trash on the left. Watson began pointing to buildings so run-down they were difficult to see. "Okay, over right in here," he said, "you used to have the Hudson County jail. And in there, whenever there was a moon tide, the cells would fill with water and the inmates would have to climb up to stay dry. . . . I have the key to this yard over here, with all the boats. We catch blue crabs in there. I eat them and now my head probably glows in the dark because back in the teens and twenties they had a hat factory in there, and they used mercury to make some felt things. . . . And this is Fish House Road, and if you dig around here you can find bottles from Norway and Sweden and all over, because they came with the fish from all over, and then they'd carry them on the turnpike and take them out west out to Morristown. Hey, where is Morristown, anyway? Ah, it doesn't matter. Now, right around here George Washington had fish chowder, and I got the recipe somewhere at home because I met a Jersey City schoolteacher—we were waiting for a tow truck or whatnot—and anyway she gave me the information and the recipe. She's long gone, of course, but I have the recipe at home somewhere in my files."

Watson cruised slowly through the ruins of the great industrial past of the Meadowlands, one arm on the steering wheel, one arm pointing out the sights. If anybody else looked down at the area from a train or a car or from a plane as the flight attendants collected the last empty plastic cups in the moments before touchdown at Newark, they would have seen a large patch of industrial blight. But here at ground zero, Watson saw grandeur: he spoke like the president of the local

chamber of former commerce. "Over there they had the Egypt-
ian Lacquer Company," he said proudly. "The lacquer for your
playing cards was made there, and back over there they
invented the system to make your telephone poles with creo-
sote. . . . There used to be towers all along the water and they
weren't guarding the jail. They were guarding the docks from
terrorists—or spies, actually. We didn't have terrorists back
then. . . . And that's the naval building. We had four hundred
rifles stolen out of there one time. Who knows what happened to 'em. . . . Okay, do you see these trees? These are Nor-
wegian oak trees. There's just a couple left, but at one time
there was one hundred and sixty of them, and they all came off
the Doris Duke estate. And supposedly the root stock is from
a Polish oak. And do you know why? Well, we're at sea level
here—pretty close to it, anyway—and these roots, they can
handle it. . . . And that building was the first Ford Motor Company in the U.S., or something like that. That was one of
Ford's first assembly buildings. This was all going to be the
first Detroit. People don't realize it but it all started right
here in Kearny, New Jersey. Just like over here. Now, during
the war, we weren't allowed to trade with Communist coun-
tries, but over in that area there was a guy who went to Russia
to buy the stuff you make mothballs with. The stuff was
called—wait a minute, wait a minute. I'll remember. It was
called paradichlorobenzene, I think. You should look that up.
Anyway, the mothball industry was centered right here in
Kearny . . ."

The next thing Watson said was, "Hold on," and when he
did I grabbed the car dashboard. He put his car in reverse and
backed down a dead-end street. Watson overpowered a security guard with a wave of authority. "I'm taking you to an
important place," he said, starting in again. "Do you see that

lot out there? That was the Manhattan Produce Yards. We called it the Melon Yards. People were out there auctioning off watermelons and the other fruits. We'd have to come down to break up gambling, fights, everything. Incidentally, this was the first piggyback train yard in the world. And now turn around. Do you see this street? That was the first concrete road in the world ever laid by a machine. It went nowhere. That was their test road. And that's true. I'm not making that up. Everything I tell you is true. Just like right there. You've heard of gypsum board. That's where they made the first gypsum board in the world. And that's why this is called Gypsum Road. . . . Back there, in those houses, a big chicken company stored all their chicken shit. . . . And here they made—what do you put on your face? Powder, that's what they made. They made talcum powder. . . . That down that way was one of those portable toilet places, and they dumped all the stuff in there. They had to be careful because they put the wrong stuff into the wrong chemicals once and there were these poisonous fumes. So the first guy goes in there and he fell down dead, and then the second guy walks over to see what's wrong with him and he falls down dead too. By the time the fourth or fifth guy comes along, he stops halfway and he sees something's wrong and they called the police and then the fire department and they came in with masks on and everything."

By now, I had lost my bearings, but it didn't matter because Watson was on autopilot, narrating the past as if it had only recently been committed. We reached the old trucking area, and he began to recall details of Meadowlands deaths. "And this is the old bridge," he went on. "Boy, I pulled a lot of bodies out here. Hey, wait a minute! Where is the concrete wall? There used to be a concrete wall down here. Guys would come out of the bar that used to be back there thinking they were on the highway and they'd hit the wall at sixty miles an hour. *Bam!* . . . And this in here was the Jersey Truck Center, JTC. It's all gone now, but it used to be the biggest in the whole United States. A lot of guys were killed right in here, and just behind it people used to sunbathe under the bridge at lunchtime and stuff. By the way, most of the landfill in the ground here was done with chromium. You're basically standing on poison right now. In fact, there used to be a scale right here for the trucks to get weighed and when it was built it was supposed to last something like fifty years. But the trucks spilled chromium on the scales and it ate through 'em. The thing was shot in about ten years . . . Up here, supposedly, a freight train sunk into the ground. And we had a guy hanging for three months right up there along the river. I remember, he was all brown like tobacco. Me and my partner, we got a call that there was a dummy or something hanging up down by the river, and we spotted him from the car. But when we got up to him and we touched him, I said, 'I don't think this is any dummy.' He was leatherized 'cause he'd been hanging in the sun for so long. I think he escaped from the lunatic asylum and he was a veteran or something. They figure he hung himself on December the seventh. The other thing is, he hung himself twice. I remember there were two marks on his neck. The first time I guess it didn't take."

Of all the old steel and concrete artifacts that rot away down in south Kearny, John Watson's favorite by far is the Pulaski Skyway, the three-and-a-half-mile-long elevated highway of blackened steel that writhes like a snake across the marshes from Jersey City to Newark. It crowns the industrial meadows; it reigns over a landscape of industry retired or retooled, of nature tested and returning in its own scrambled order. If it were a statue of a man, it would have one foot in an old dump in Jersey City and one foot in Newark's dying industrial neighborhood, and it would have its hands outstretched beneath the muttony sky that seems to haunt the land beneath the Skyway. The deck of the Skyway rises to cross the river, but there is one ramp in the middle that descends down to south Kearny, as if it has lost faith in the trip. It is at the bottom of that ramp that Watson usually puts his station wagon in park and says something along the lines of, "So, what do you want to know?"

What I already knew about the Skyway was that it is the greatest in a long history of better ways built to cross a land that has always made travel difficult if not precarious. In pre-Revolutionary times, people in New Jersey traveled more than people in any other colony—New Jersey's reputation as a state with numerous and technologically advanced roads pre-dates the construction of the New Jersey Turnpike—but roads in the Meadowlands mostly went around swamp. Ferries and sailboats took passengers from New York to Newark via Jersey City, and it was not unusual for papers to report that a ship making the trip had been blown out to sea and never been seen again. The first road across the meadows was proposed in 1765 by the New Jersey legislature. It was constructed with logs from the remaining cedar forest, and it was notoriously rough; passengers sat on hard wooden seats and often held on to one another to prevent themselves from bouncing to the stagecoach floor (spring-loaded seats were introduced in 1766). Despite its texture, the road was well reviewed. "Built wholly of wood with much care and perseverance," wrote one traveler on the old corduroy road, "in the midst of water, on a soil that trembles under your feet, it proves to what point may be carried that patience of man, who is determined to conquer nature." Railroads eventually conquered the meadows. Tracks were put down on cedar logs, or in some cases trash; after the tracks were laid on the meadows, it was not considered safe to travel on them until a year had passed and they were less likely to sink. The Paterson and Hudson River Railroad hired William Gibbs McNeill and George Washington Whistler to design the first pan-meadows track. Horses drew a train called the McNeill across for the first time in 1833. (Whistler went on to marry McNeill's sister, and their son, James Abbott McNeill Whistler, used her as his model for *Mother*.) If the train derailed and became mired in the swamp, passengers were expected to help put the train back on the tracks. Sometimes passengers would stop the train on the meadows, and the engineer would wait while people hunted turtles. After a while, there were numerous ferries and railroad bridges and some drawbridges for automobiles, but the Skyway was planned in the 1920s, a time when people in New York City were in the middle of an economic boom and they wanted to drive out of their newly completed Holland Tunnel and get to the west fast. The Meadowlands blocked the path to the rest of America like a big pothole. The thirteen-mile trip from Jersey City across the Meadowlands and through Newark was full of old roads and drawbridges and it could take two and a half hours. This was the most time-consuming gap on the Lincoln Highway that went from New York to Washington, D.C., and was then the most traveled highway in the world.

The approach to the design of the Skyway was similar to the approach that children used to take in crossing the meadows using two planks, which is to say that plans were drawn up as construction went along. To be sunk into the bedrock, piles had to pass through 147 feet of muck, a record depth for pneumatic drilling at the time. The job required two million rivets—sometimes the Skyway looks as if it is made only of rivets—and 88,461 tons of steel, which was more steel than was used in the construction of the George Washington Bridge. The Skyway is part elevated highway, part bridge, and if you're driving over it you know you are on the bridge part when you feel as though you are entering the black-ribbed belly of a whale. One of the engineers who designed the Skyway was Sven Hedin. Hedin, a robust man, had learned bridge engineering in Sweden. He was known for not being concerned with minutiae, and when he looked over plans for the Skyway, he had a habit of allowing the ash on his cigarette to grow so long that it was unbearable for his colleagues. Aside from building bridges, Hedin was very interested in learning the English language. Every day, during the construction of the Skyway, he would work *The Times* crossword puzzle on his lunch break in an endeavor to improve his vocabulary. Hedin enjoyed telling the other engineers about the time he went into Manhattan with his wife and daughter to see a play and have dinner and he narrowly avoided being duped. After dinner, while drinking coffee with anisette, Hedin happened to notice the last item on his bill, which said, "If it works—$2." He called the waiter over and, in his thick Scandinavian accent, asked the waiter what the last line meant. The waiter shrugged his shoulders, crossed off the last line, and said, "It didn't work."

Fifteen men died while building the Skyway, and one man was murdered. The man who was murdered was a casualty of a labor war that occurred during construction. The dispute was called The War of the Meadows. The War of the Meadows was really a struggle between Theodore Brandle and Frank Hague. Brandle was a millionaire labor leader who led a troop of ironworkers. Brandle's ironworkers picketed the

Skyway construction because one of the steel contractors paid steelworkers two dollars below union wages, sixteen dollars a day. Frank Hague was the last of America's great political bosses. He was known as Frank "I Am the Law" Hague. It is said that in Jersey City, under the reign of Hague, not only did the dead vote in elections but, because of a law that allowed people to vote in party primaries regardless of party affiliation, the dead voted twice. Hague boasted that Jersey City had the lowest crime rate in the nation, but he could say that only because many activities illegal elsewhere were not against the law in Jersey City. In fact, gambling was encouraged by the mayor, so much so that Jersey City was nicknamed "the Bourse of the Horse." Hague grew up poor but while mayor lived in a mansion in Jersey City and had homes in Atlantic City and Florida and drove through the Holland Tunnel to eat lunch in Manhattan at the Plaza Hotel just about every day. He was a perfect tyrant. In 1938, when *Life* magazine published what he considered to be an unflattering photograph of him, he had every copy of the issue removed from Jersey City newspaper stands. He owned part of two of the three papers in Jersey City, and he employed the editor of the third paper as the state historian. Hague considered one of his great achievements to be the construction of a local maternity hospital, which he named the Margaret Hague Maternity Hospital, after his mother. When he spoke of the hospital, his droopy blue eyes welled with tears.

During The War of the Meadows, the steel company shuttled workers to the Skyway construction sites on river barges or hidden in trucks. The strikers stood on the old Lincoln Highway bridge and protested by throwing bottles and bolts and rocks. Eventually, a mob of union men met a carload of nonunion workers on one of the unfinished Skyway ramps and attacked them. Thirty-eight-year-old Thomas Harrison had his skull broken—he was beaten with a pipe—and the next day he died, leaving a wife and two children. The nonunion workers who had been at the scene of the attack said they didn't think that they could recognize the union men who had attacked them if the union men were put in a police lineup, so Hague dispatched his police force to take care of the strikers and in so doing ended Brandle's career. Hague was quoted as saying, "[G]et those responsible no matter where the trail leads." He added, "We don't give our cops nightsticks for ornaments." Although Hague once embraced the labor union and its leader—Brandle had proposed that Hague be elected for life—Hague now decided Brandle was no longer his ally, and he sided with the forces behind the construction of the Skyway.

Hague didn't realize that huge federal highway projects like the Skyway signaled the end of the power of his political pork. He decided to make sure it would be built. "Police were ordered today to wage relentless war against Brandle gang rioters," the *Jersey City Journal* reported. "This order is understood to have come direct from Mayor Hague with the injunction to 'disregard Brandle . . . or anybody else.' " Brandle attempted to negotiate a settlement to The War of the Meadows by visiting Hague but Hague would not see him. Hague said, "Teddy, get out of here. I've washed my hands of you." Soon, Brandle would be displaced from his post. Meanwhile, one of the union men accused in the murder, James Byrne, a thirty-six-year-old from Weehawken, went into hiding in Pennsylvania. Another union worker was apprehended a few months after the murder. The jailed union worker was William "Star" Campbell, a twenty-two-year-old out-of-work prizefighter from Jersey City. Coincidentally, Campbell's wife was one of the first women admitted to Margaret Hague

Maternity Hospital during the first week it opened. Campbell himself had broken his wrist on the way to the hospital to be with his wife—he'd cranked a friend's car engine and the engine kicked back. When he finally got to the hospital, his wife died while giving birth to her tenth child. She was the first woman to die in the Margaret Hague Maternity Hospital. After his wife died, to support his children, Campbell was given temporary work with the city, which kept him occupied for a few days until he was offered picket duty. When he found himself in jail accused of murder, he tore off the sleeve from his old raincoat and tried to hang himself but failed. The next day, Hague had Campbell taken from his cell and charged with attempted suicide.

On the day the Skyway officially opened, November 23, 1932, elected officials from New York and New Jersey swarmed to the meadows. They praised the Skyway and they praised the development of the Meadowlands, which they hoped the Skyway would help transform from marsh to fields filled with factories. In a sea of fedoras, Thomas H. McDonald, head of the Federal Bureau of Roads, called it "the greatest highway ever built." At the site of the celebration, the waters from New York's Hudson and East Rivers were mixed with the waters of the Passaic and Hackensack, as if in sacrifice to the gods of progress. "Now," proclaimed *The Times*, "there is a viaduct, cutting almost as the airplane flies, from the mouth of the Holland Tunnel." Complaints about the twenty-one-million-dollar cost of the Skyway were soothed by the statistical justification offered by the traffic engineers. The old two-and-a-half-hour trip from Jersey City through Newark now took fifteen minutes. To exploit this timesaving, traffic engineers invented a kind of inverse statistic—VMS, or vehicle miles saved. The Bureau of Roads estimated the exact amount of time the Skyway would save drivers each year, and the newspapers listed the numbers like winning scores: 57,445,000 VMS for cars; 4,883,000 VMS for light trucks; 3,827,000 VMS for heavy trucks. Thanks to VMS the Skyway made citizens money before their cars left the garage. "The commission has calculated," the *Herald Tribune* reported, "that this will save persons and firms operating motor vehicles another $134,000,000." The Skyway was America's first superhighway, and in the efficient land of all future super-highways, progress yielded only future profits, never costs— the Skyway was a one-way street.

And yet almost the very day after it was opened, the Sky-way was impractical. Trucks were banned from the Skyway, and in light of the number of head-on collisions, engineers had to sacrifice one timesaving lane for the construction of a miniature Skyway-long wall—an aluminium hybrid of the inverted Y-shaped highway barricade that in its concrete form is known nationally as the Jersey Barrier. (It had to be alu-minum because the Skyway couldn't withstand the weight of so much concrete, though once during World War II a lane of the Skyway was used to store tanks for the army.) The Skyway was and still is impractical because it is scary, and with good reason: a Hudson County police officer once told me, "If you break down up there, you can pretty much count on being hit." People all around the New York metropolitan area avoid the Pulaski Skyway, taking the wide and monotonous New Jersey Turnpike instead and so missing out on what the mayor of Newark described as a "spiritual fixture."

Whenever I drive the Skyway, I feel like I'm driving on a narrow-gauge roller coaster that has been flattened out into a racetrack for commuter traffic. To pass another driver in the thin air of the Skyway seems death-defying, a legitimate feat.

The Skyway was named in honor of General Casmir Pulaski, a Polish nobleman who was exiled after being wrongly accused of plotting against King Stanislaus, and while driving the Skyway I have always taken personal satisfaction in knowing that General Pulaski, who was described as dashing, with blond hair and a well-waxed mustache, frequently undertook what one biographer called "typically aggressive charges." According to one account, "His special stunt was to fire his pistol while at a full gallop, toss it into the air, catch it, and hurl it at an imaginary enemy ahead. With one foot in the stirrup, and his horse still galloping, Pulaski would then swing to the ground and pick up the gun." He died in 1779, two days after leading an attack on massed artillery in Georgia.

Once, John Watson waited near one of the Skyway's off-ramps for a shipment of gold bullion to be stolen—the police were in on the planned heist. "The shipment was going somewhere to somewhere," he said. "I forget. It was all secret. But we waited for these crooks and then they stole the wrong trucks." On another occasion, Watson rescued a seventy-five-year-old man from one of the Skyway's supports. The man's mind had faded and he had thought he was in a subway station descending toward a bathroom; he suddenly found himself over the Passaic River. The wind was so strong that day that all maintenance work had been called off, but Watson climbed out and pulled the man to safety.

Watson told me some of these stories the times I saw him in the Skyway Diner, a restaurant located directly beneath the Skyway where he works part-time as a handyman. We'd talk for a while and then drive back to his home. On the way back, we always passed Barczewski Street, a little road that ends in a blur of reeds at the northernmost edge of the Kearny Marsh.

Each time, Watson spoke cryptically about the murder he investigated there, saying only things like "She was a beautiful girl" or "I don't like to talk about that," which was not something you usually heard from him. When I pressed him, he would change the subject, elaborating instead on the old Du Pont factory, for instance, and about how it was equipped with holes in the floor that technicians jumped into when an experiment seemed ready to explode. After a while, though, I pieced the story together.

Nicole DeCombe disappeared in January of 1983. She was twenty-three years old and her friends called her Nikki. She was the stepdaughter of a lawyer who practiced international law in New York and lived not far from Kearny, in Montclair. She had left home when she was sixteen and lived at the homes of relatives and friends. Her boyfriend, twenty-four-year-old José Machado, pumped gas in Union City and lived in Jersey City with his parents, who immigrated to the United States from Cuba in 1966. DeCombe's friends later testified that Machado was extremely jealous of her; once, they said, he dragged her out of the bar in the Meadowlands Sports Complex where she worked as a waitress because he had found her outfit too revealing. A few months before she disappeared, she had become pregnant. She considered marrying Machado but then aborted the baby against his wishes. DeCombe ended the relationship. When she disappeared, the police searched the Meadowlands until a storm buried the area in two feet of snow. Her body was discovered during a brief thaw in February. A fireman was out birding in Kearny with his children and came across the woman's decomposed body. Her hands were bound behind her and she had been stabbed twenty times in the back.

Watson was one of the detectives on the case, and he traveled to libraries all over northern New Jersey reading books on knots and eventually matched the knot used to tie the hands of DeCombe to a knot commonly used to tie bales of sugarcane on farms in Cuba. He searched the towns around the Meadowlands for stores that sold the kind of pocketknife used in the murder; he would park his car and walk for a mile or so in every direction, interviewing every store owner, and then drive to another town and repeat the task over and over again. Watson and the other detectives on the case all suspected Machado, but they couldn't pin anything on him. Machado said he was innocent, that DeCombe had jumped out of his car after an argument, that she had told him she was walking home. The FBI sent an agent who was an expert in psychological portraits of killers. The agent was a former Kearny high school English teacher. Watson still speaks enthusiastically about this man. "This guy was amazing," Watson said one day as we stood at the end of Barczewski Street, a few yards from where the body was found. "He came down here and I showed him everything—where the body was, how it was found. He just took it all in. Then, I just left him alone and he just looked around and concentrated. A couple of days later, I had this profile and it said basically that it was a crime of passion. That was the thing about the stab wounds. I think they were in a circle and one thing they say is that when you have knife wounds in a circle like that it tends to be a crime of passion."

Then, one day, Watson noticed that a rope attached to a garage door at the gas station where Machado worked was similar to the rope that bound the hands of the young girl. Police chemists later matched green paint chips found in a pair of Machado's coveralls with green paint chips discovered on the rope found with DeCombe's body on the end of Barczewski

Street. This evidence was enough to have Machado arrested, tried, convicted, and sentenced to life in jail in 1984, but three years later he was released on bail. His conviction was overturned in a precedent-setting appeal. (The prosecution used undated letters DeCombe had written to friends saying she feared her jealous boyfriend and the state supreme court ruled that such hearsay could not be used to show the victim's state of mind.) In anticipation of a second trial, Machado pleaded guilty to manslaughter to minimize the amount of time he might spend in jail—he was married by now, with a child. But the plea was thrown out; a new trial was scheduled and Watson was called out of retirement to testify. Finally, in 1995, Machado was acquitted at his second trial. Machado's attorney argued that evidence had been collected improperly and incompletely by Kearny detectives twelve years earlier.

Watson grimaced. "They said I should have used gloves," he said. We got back in his car. "When I picked up the knife, they said I should have used gloves to do it, but it didn't make a difference either way. It didn't matter. And besides, nobody was using gloves then. That was a long time ago."

I felt bad about asking to hear his story. I felt as if I'd convinced him to tell me a secret that I didn't want to know. For his part, Watson eventually became more at ease discussing the case with me and later he would show me his files and newspaper clippings describing the search for the girl's body and he would say again, "She was a beautiful girl." But in that moment, as we started up the hill back to his house from Barczewski Street, I felt as if I'd touched on a frustration related to more than just this one case, this one body of all the bodies in the Meadowlands that Watson had ever come across. In the car, as he stared out the windshield, I asked him if he missed being a detective. When I did, he stopped the car and looked at me and it was as if I had asked him the meaning of life.

"I miss it to this day, to this minute," he said. "And do you know why? Because it takes you a long time to accumulate the knowledge."

He pointed out the car. "Like for instance," he continued, "look over there at that building, that warehouse. See how one door is open and one door looks like it's closed up. Now, what I'll do is store that. Keep it in my head. And see that sign over there in front of that building? You remember that. You remember that because you may need it someday. It may be useful. You accumulate the knowledge. Do you see what I mean? And then all of a sudden you're supposed to just stop."

He shook his head and started the car moving again, driving slowly up out of the swamp, up the hill. "The thing is, you just can't," he said.

The Trapper
and the Fisherman

ON AN OVERCAST SUMMER DAY, WITH A THICK SHEET OF GRAY
clouds crawling over the low flat bottom of the Hackensack
River Valley, at Eagan's, a steak and seafood place across from
a dump and a marsh and a couple of highways, two local
Meadowlands celebrities sat together for the very first time.
The man from Secaucus, Bill Sheehan, arrived first. Sheehan,
forty-eight, is heavyset and of medium height, and he wears a
thick gray mustache that looks like something off an ancient
mariner and contributes to his overall nautical look—his
nickname is Captain Bill. On that afternoon, he wore a black
leather vest, a white cap, and white T-shirt, both decorated
with the logo of the Hackensack Estuaries and River Tender
Corporation, or HEART, the organization he founded. Sheehan
works in Jersey City as a taxi dispatcher, and he had driven

across the meadows and through the valley of old dumps in his beat-up old station wagon. Now, at Eagan's, he swaggered to a dark booth in the back and said of his lunch companion, "I'll bet you he doesn't come."

Despite this prediction, Don Smith arrived a few minutes later. Smith is a naturalist with the Hackensack Meadowlands Development Commission. Fifty-two years old, he is tall and muscular, with a rugged complexion and shaggy dark brown hair only just turning gray. He had driven a big state-owned pickup truck from just a mile up the meadows where the office he is rarely in overlooks the Kingsland Marsh, and he walked into the restaurant looking as if he were in the middle of something. The night before he too had made a prediction about *his* lunch companion today. "I'll bet he doesn't show," he said. But now Smith put his walkie-talkie down on the table and greeted Sheehan cordially, if bluntly, as he does when they occasionally pass each other giving tours on the Meadowlands' waterways.

On the river, after they pass each other, their smiles tend to sink fast, like a cement-filled fifty-five-gallon drum. A few weeks before, as he cruised into an old creek in Secaucus, Sheehan had this to say about Smith: "I'll tell you, I feel bad for Don Smith. He's a good naturalist. He knows the river better than me. He's a better birder than me. I'm not ashamed to admit it. But I didn't do what he did. I didn't sell out and go to work for the state." Meanwhile, the very night before, Smith said this about Sheehan: "As it is now, I work for a state agency, so I've got to keep myself under control, but I'm getting ready to retire, and when I do, I'm probably gonna punch that guy in the nose."

While some people consider the notion of a Meadowlands environmentalist an oxymoron, there are actually two envi-

ronmentalists running around the Meadowlands, and they
don't get along. At Eagan's, Smith took the chicken breast,
Sheehan had beef.

For a long time, environmentalists were nearly extinct in the
Meadowlands, and Don Smith was a rare breed. He came to
the HMDC in 1970 from the Bronx Zoo, where he worked as
a zookeeper with aquatic birds. He began as a volunteer and
then became a naturalist at the HMDC. His first charge was
to reintroduce the people of New Jersey to the Hackensack
River, which for the past hundred years or so the people of
New Jersey had mistaken for a sewer, and he has been relentless in this reintroduction for nearly thirty years. In undertak-
ing this task, Smith considers his life spent trapping on the
Meadowlands to be his greatest credential. Smith grew up in
Little Ferry, on the north end of the meadows, eating meals
with pig farm—salvaged silverware that had the Waldorf-
Astoria's markings on it. He began trapping when he was
fourteen. Muskrat traps were traded as gifts in school at
Christmastime in Little Ferry. When the school bus dropped
him at home, Smith would wander into the meadows around
Losen Slote with his rifle on his shoulder and his Chesapeake
retriever leading the way. Neighbors placed orders for pheasant or rabbits as he passed their houses. In time, he joined the
ranks of the great trappers of the Meadowlands, the so-called
meadow rats, who trapped muskrats each winter in the 1940s
and 1950s at a time when the pelts of the muskrats of the
Meadowlands were rivaled only by those of Ohio and northern New York State. Other meadow rats included: Jacob
Kraft, who was once known as the mayor of the Meadows,
and lived in a house that he built on land that is roughly
where the Meadowlands Sports Complex is now; Charlie

Lanza, who occasionally caught platinum blond muskrats in Overpeck Creek meadow, where Liz Claiborne is based now; and Willie Royka, who once caught three thousand rats in a season. Don Smith learned trapping from a meadow rat by the name of Pete Mavis. In November 1950, a Nor'wester broke the dikes along Saw Mill Creek and the phragmites marsh was inundated with salt water. This made for a muskrat paradise, and guys like Pete Mavis were in heaven. "Pete used to say that you could step from one muskrat hut to another," Smith remembered. Local muskrats reacted with similar reproductive enthusiasm in the sixties when the New Jersey Turnpike extension impounded three hundred acres of Kearny Marsh. Smith fondly remembers this time himself. By this time, he was a teenager and local fur buyers were dropping by his home to buy pelts for the going rate, which was $2 apiece at the time. Smith once caught a record 129 pelts in one day. Perhaps his most enduring contribution to local trapping tradition was the use of stakes to identify individuals' traps, which significantly reduced muskrat trap crimes. "So much thievery went on," Smith remembered. In time, Tommy Hart from Kearny had a maroon stake; Leo Lowry had a notched stake—he was considered the last of the great trap thieves—and Louie Crecco trapped with black-and-yellow stakes and then threw his rats in the back of his Cadillac on top of which he kept his canoe. Smith said, "The stakes brought peace to the valley."

Aside from Smith, one of the last muskrat trappers in the Meadowlands is eighty-three-year-old George Schilling, whom I ran into one crisp fall day when I was wandering around in the Kingsland Marsh. Schilling has white hair and an impish grin, and if I hadn't known he was a trapper I might have guessed he was lost and looking for a workshop in the vicinity of the North Pole. On the day I ran into him, he was wearing a red plaid shirt, brown corduroys, and hip waders. Schilling was leery of me at first because people protesting muskrat trapping in the Meadowlands had recently slashed his car's tires. But after a while, he let me look into the big wicker basket he carried on his back: it was filled with muskrats. The muskrats had long thick black tails and long yellow teeth that were curved like uncut fingernails. "There aren't many rats left anymore," Schilling said. "If you want to make money, you're better off working at McDonald's. I just do it for sport." Shilling spoke highly of Don Smith. He recalled that Smith had analyzed a few of the muskrats he had caught in the Kearny Marsh at a time when muskrats began dying there for no apparent reason.

Smith is the closest thing to a park ranger the Meadowlands has. The HMDC is stocked with wildlife biologists and plant specialists, but Smith spends his days riding around on the old dumps, out in his pontoon boats, and at various meetings, where he discusses the Meadowlands' future and its past. He also spends a lot of time monitoring what's natural and what's not. When he started at the HMDC, Smith identified and helped clean up the ponds of cyanide that once existed out in the meadows. "I always wondered why all those green ponds had no life in 'em—no mosquitoes, nothing," he said. Once, he put a man in jail for fouling a creek. More recently, he has worked to build a nature trail that runs the length of the Meadowlands, following a natural gas pipeline that in turn follows the path of the western spur of the New Jersey Turnpike Extension as it follows the path of the Hackensack.

Smith is best known for leading tours down the Hackensack River and its creeks and streams, and these tours have begun to sell out weeks in advance. I managed to sneak into one on a summer night. The sky was clear and the tide was high, and a dozen people climbed on his boat as it started up at its dock in Secaucus, just north of the Hess oil tanks and across from Exit 18W on the New Jersey Turnpike. With Smith were three young children, a newly married couple, and several retirees. "This is beautiful down here, and nobody knows," a woman whispered to me. "You tell people you're going out on the Hackensack and they laugh and say, Oh *sure!*" Smith stood behind the wheel of the boat, commanding the attention of the little group with his grouchy enthusiasm. As he took off south down the Hackensack, he pointed out a recent housing development in Secaucus, shaking his head. "We felt if we could get people to live next to the river, they'd rediscover the river," he said, "and it worked so well that now they formed an organization to oppose any further development. They don't want anybody else to live here." Next came an old landfill. He explained that it was a trash reef, with old refuse gradually eroding into the river, until the trash was covered and secured with rocks that a local contractor was looking to get rid of—this being an example of the kind of pro-active ecological management that characterizes Smith's Meadowlands philosophy. "That's the kind of thing we like to do," he said. "Solve two problems at one time."

As the sky grew red and became tictactoed with bands of purple contrails, as the hotels one by one lit their twenty-story-high neon red lights over the filled-in portions of the Meadowlands, the tour wound into the marshes off Penhorn Creek, just south of Snake Hill, on the border between industrial meadow and less industrial meadow. The boat became momentarily mired in mud and Smith had to use a pole to push it out. The highlight of the tour was in the Kingsland Marsh. We floated through the spartina-fringed mouth of

Saw Mill Creek, and Smith became wildly animated, as if he'd
just come home from school again and was heading out with
his dog. "There's a red-winged blackbird. There's some cormorants, an egret, and that's a green-winged teal," he said. A
dozen heads whipped around. "And *Ooooooh boy!*" he continued. "Big fish! Right there on the edge of the spartina. He got
something, I'd say." He turned to look elsewhere and said,
"Now, that's a pretty sight over there." He cupped his hands:
"Heeeeeeeeyyyy-Aiii!" A heron stretched his wings to see who
was calling. "I went in Sunday into the interior of that area
and put up nine great blue herons with a song," Smith added
with pride. "There's some night heron there, too." He pointed
east and said, "Okay, here are three great blues, coming right
at us from the Empire State Building. Okay, look at that!"

As opposed to being the riverkeeper for the neighboring Hudson River, a job that is considered to be that of environmental
avenger and that garners considerable positive press, the general perception of the poor health of the Hackensack causes the
Hackensack Riverkeeper's job to be perceived as akin to night
watchman at a funeral home. Consequently, Bill Sheehan
relishes small victories. Recently, Sheehan fought successfully
for the Hackensack's inclusion on the threatened rivers list
released annually by a group called American Rivers. This
was covered as big news in *HEART-BEAT,* his organization's
newsletter, the thinking being that the inclusion might win
him some more funding via small private grants. "Needless to
say, I am pleased that the Hackensack River made the list," he
wrote in his column, "Captain's Corner." Sheehan leads what
he considers a rival tour to Smith's; he refers to his journeys
through the Meadowlands as eco-tours, in the environmental
lingo of the day. One day I took one of Sheehan's eco-tours. I

thought it was going to be ponderous and National Geographic special-like, but it had the good-natured feel of an
afternoon on a fishing boat and I found myself hankering for a
beer.

Sheehan grew up on the high ground of Secaucus when the
Meadowlands Parkway was a salt marsh and young Secaucus
hunters leaned their shotguns against the outside wall of the
area's delicatessen. Fishing is his passion, even though most
Meadowlands fish are eaten cautiously if at all. "I'm a fisherman," he often says. "I'm not, you know, book taught. I know
what I know from being here. I mean, if you had told me ten
years ago that I'd be out here on the river talking about land
use policy, I'd have said, *Yeah, right!*' In a perfect world scenario, I'd be taking people up and down the river all day and
then at the end of the day I'd do a little fishing." Unfortunately, because of HEART and because he is chairman of
Secaucus's environmental advisory committee, he has little
time for fishing. And now he thinks not just of the river but
all the water in the Meadowlands. "I heard a guy on the radio
the other day and he said, 'And if you believe that, I've got
some land I'd like to sell you in the Meadowlands.' And I
thought, *What's wrong with that?* I'd love some land out there.
You know? I'd preserve it."

I met Sheehan for a boat ride in Carlstadt one day, at the
dock behind the Golf Center that he calls his home port; he
was just wrapping up an eco-tour with a group of Cub Scouts
and the finale had him pulling a fish line off the end of the pier.
On the end was a catfish covered in slime that clearly wanted
back in the Hackensack. Sheehan was saying, "See, there *are*
things living in this river." A huge cloud of black smoke hung
nearby over the East Rutherford meadows, because a fire had
broken out in the reeds: fire trucks screamed down dirt roads

across filled land. Sheehan headed north, away from the fire, toward Mill Creek in Secaucus.

As we cruised up the Hackensack, Sheehan talked about local hawks with chemicals in their bloodstream, about the new sewer treatment plant in Secaucus, and he laid out his ecological management philosophy for the Meadowlands, which favors educational endeavors and an end to water pollution and is generally hands-off. The HMDC supports some development plans in the Meadowlands—a new shopping mall in Carlstadt, a fun park in East Rutherford, fourteen thousand new residential units, and a total of thirty million new square feet of combined office, manufacturing, and warehouse space; it maintains that careful development of a few areas can support the rehabilitation of other areas of wetlands. Sheehan, on the other hand, thinks the Meadowlands are overdeveloped already, and of the little less than eight thousand acres of wetlands left, his group would like to see them all preserved. Sheehan's environmental philosophy with regard to the Meadowlands clashes most severely with that of the HMDC's on the issue of phragmites, the ubiquitous reed that is the modern Meadowlands' most prevalent species. The HMDC believes that phragmites are of little food value to the creatures, small and microscopic, at the bottom of the long food chain that begins in the estuary, that phragmites serve only to raise the ground level of the marsh, turn it into non-marsh, into dry ground. The staff at the HMDC are fond of saying, as are many environmentalists, that a salt marsh produces more food than any other habitat on earth. In a study done in 1981, the HMDC compared the number of creatures inhabiting a square food of spartina marsh and a square foot of phragmites marsh and found the population in the spartina marsh outnumbered that in the phragmites marsh 1,527 to 321. The HMDC wants to destroy acres of phragmites in the Meadowlands and plant spartina, and in fact, they have planted pockets of it with some success. Sheehan argues the phragmites are home to significant wildlife on their own and ought to be left as is. "I mean, all these bureaucrats who want to tell the river what to do," he said, shaking his head. "If the river's coming back on its own, then who am I to question the river? You get where I'm going?"

On the boat trip that afternoon, he took me to an area that had recently been planted with spartina and showed me where some of the grass had died. He started spinning. "This is what the HMDC calls the mitigation site. In a lot of places, the spartina didn't take. My theory is that it must be some kind of a genetic imprint thing," he said. "In other words, what I'm saying is, if you take a spartina grass from a more pristine area and you put it in here, the spartina grass is gonna say, 'What did I do?' And then it's gonna die." Later he added, "Now, you ask me, how can I know this stuff if I'm just a fisherman. I don't have an M.S. or a B.S. or an M.B.A. I'm just a fisherman. But they should make it part of their requirement in school to go out with me, go out with Captain Bill. I don't want to sound egotistical or anything, but they should all have to go out with someone like me. For example, I was out with this scientist and she was told that Mill Creek in Secaucus was a dead creek. So I brought her out here and there were lots of birds happening. And she says to me, 'I was told this was a dead creek.' So basically after she went out with me, she knew that she had been bullshitted."

When Smith and Sheehan finally sat down together at Eagan's, Sheehan began to chitchat about the river and make pronouncements such as "I'm just a grassroots group here," refer-

ring to the river not as a river but as a "resource." Sheehan
referred to Smith by the nickname "Donny." For his part,
Smith sat back in his chair, looking irritated and playing with
his fork. He knew he was about to come under attack. For a few
minutes, the two managed to chat amiably. They were both
happy that large chunks of the Meadowlands are now being
bought up by the Hackensack River Conservancy, for instance,
a move intended to preserve the region's open space. "This is
where we coalesce," Sheehan said. And they both talked shop
about the joys of leading people through the Meadowlands.

"People say, Jesus, we didn't know there was this much life
here," Sheehan said. "And then when you turn around there is
the World Trade Center. *That* impresses people."

"I describe it as an urban wilderness," Smith said.

"Exactly," Sheehan said.

But when the conversation turned to phragmites, Sheehan
took it as an opportunity to strike out. "Okay," he said. "Now
let me give you some counterpoint, Donny. And now I'm not
going to give you this coming from me but I'm gonna refer to
this document here." Sheehan pulled a two-inch-thick report
from his briefcase and brandished it like a sword. Smith
remained slouched in his chair, unperturbed. "This document
right here," Sheehan continued, "which was prepared by the
United States Environmental Protection Agency, says"—he
flipped to a marked page and read—"that loss of phragmites
habitat to development would reduce, let's see, breeding, nesting, and feeding habitat for numerous lowland species, elimi-
nating year-round habitat for waterfowl and non-migratory
birds such as moorhens, rails and bitterns; eliminate or
severely reduce deep water habitat for fish species, and would
eliminate the source of valuable detrital substrate essential to
the Meadowlands estuarine eco-system." Sheehan looked at

Smith as if to say, *Aha!* He sat back, his arm across the back of Eagan's booth. "Now, I didn't make that up, Donny."

Smith didn't miss a beat. He leaned forward, pointed his fork at Sheehan, and looked straight in the fisherman's eyes. "And Bill," he said, speaking slowly and forcefully, "I'll blow it full of holes." He punctuated this statement by adding, "It is not worth the paper it is written on.

"Know how they counted the birds, Bill?"

"I've read the whole thing, Don. I . . ."

"How'd they count the birds?"

Smith was still leaning forward across the table. Sheehan attempted to blunt Smith's attack by taking a sarcastic approach. "Oh, okay, Don," Sheehan said, "tell us how they counted the birds."

"I'll tell you how they counted the birds," Smith said. He was still jabbing at the air with his fork. "They approached the mitigation site, scared 'em out. Counted 'em, and meanwhile all the birds have flown up to the phragmites marsh. Then they go up in their boat to the phragmites marsh and they count the same birds in there and they say the number of birds in the two places are equal. I mean, of course the number is *equal!* Show me the food, Bill. Show me the food in the phragmites marsh. There isn't any. There's nothing."

Smith was on a roll. "And as for moorhens," he said, "you ever hunt moorhens, Bill?"

"No, I've never hunted them."

"Well, there are damn few moorhens in the Meadowlands anymore. And least bitterns. I haven't seen a least bittern in two years, Bill. *Two years!*"

Sheehan was barely holding his ground until the conversation turned to discussion of a pocket of meadows that had recently been purchased by Secaucus with the intention of keeping it open space. "Now that none of that area is going to be developed, if we don't intervene, if we leave it the way it is, it's all going downhill," Don Smith said.

Sheehan interjected, taking his I'm-just-a-fisherman tack again. "Now, that's something that we maybe shouldn't discuss," he said. "That's something that maybe the biologists should discuss."

"But Bill," said Smith, as the man with all the expertise, "we've brought in the top experts in the country and they agree with us—they agree with that point one hundred percent."

Sheehan paused to regroup. "Don, since I began associating with the kind of people I've been associating with lately— experts and scientists and that kind of person—I've started thinking about the river—geological time and stuff. And one thing I've started to realize is that a human life is like a blink of an eye to this river. And for us to stand on the banks of the river and do the Moses thing and tap the phragmites three times with the rod and expect the river to do what we want, it's kind of like an imposition of our human values."

"But hey," Smith said, "we tampered with it already. In simple terms, we broke it—we gotta to fix it. We're not moving into some pristine area here. And this is the biggest gripe I got with a lot of the people you're associated with—that they stand up and say let it take its course. But *we're the ones who screwed it up!* And the information on the table says that in the areas that the system needs help because of misguided decisions our ancestors made, we've got to intervene."

The waitress was pouring coffee when Sheehan tried a conciliatory tack. "I know what you mean," he said. "That's why I'm involved in this in the first place. This is an area that with a little bit of management and with a great deal of loving care could turn into a fish-producing habitat."

This remark seemed to please Smith, or at least it didn't visibly perturb him. He sat back. Then he asked Sheehan one last question.

"Tell me, Bill," he said, very calmly. "Why do you think the water quality in the Meadowlands is better today than it was twenty years ago? Name the single biggest reason."

Sheehan was wary. He rose carefully to take the bait.

"Why do I think it's better today?" Sheehan repeated slowly. "Well, let's see, there's sea level rise." Sheehan then mentioned the elimination of widespread garbage dumping, the implementation of sewage treatment plants. Smith shook his head at each response. Finally, Sheehan said, "Okay, I give up, Don. What's the single biggest reason the river is cleaner? You tell me."

"The single biggest reason the river is cleaner is because of the HMDC."

"*Ohhhh,* okay, Don. Is *that* what you were waiting for me to say?"

With this, things began to get a little out of hand. Don Smith was really worked up and Bill Sheehan seemed to be aggravating him, so I changed the subject.

Later, after the check was paid, I was getting into my rental car and Bill Sheehan took me aside and said, "You see what I mean about him?"

I didn't hear from Don Smith until a couple of weeks later, when he responded by postcard to a wildlife question I had asked him. In the postcard, he said this: "Bill Sheehan and group are still at their lies and deceptions. Too bad I can only deal from the top of the deck."

"Not to dwell on it, but these are the guys who, one of them, at a meeting, he says, 'I'm not gonna be happy until I can

stand on the shore of the Hackensack and see the same thing
that the Indians saw.' And I mean, that's just not gonna happen." This is what Don Smith was saying to me on a cold
autumn morning as we walked around the top of an old landfill in Kearny. This particular landfill used to be a burning
dump. It burned for about a decade. The fire was extinguished and the garbage was covered with dirt that was
trucked in from New York City, from a lot where a parking
structure was being built. "It was beautiful clean soil," Smith
said. The organic component of the soil was boosted by
adding compost donated by nearby Teaneck, New Jersey.
Rutgers conducted planting experiments on the old dump.
"Now you don't see an old garbage dump off the turnpike,"
Smith said. "You see a beautiful meadow on a hill. And that
helps the image of New Jersey, too. If you didn't do this, it
would just be a race between phragmites and wormwood. So
you have to jump-start the system. Someday, these wooded
areas will spread and there will be a future decision to make.
Should we hold the forest here? I want to put some red berries
in here as well, for the birds." We got in his truck and drove
along a trail so overgrown that the front seat was dark when
we hit a big patch. He pointed out the window. "There's a
pretty grass. Bluestem. In the sunlight, it looks amber."

In Smith's vision, in the new Meadowlands, the garbage-
hilled swamp is transformed into an upland habitat, a place
where the species that once lived in the hills that were taken
over by towns and cities are able to take up again and prosper.
There are trees and shrubs on the garbage hills in the new
Meadowlands, and rocks are brought in to create ledges and
even caves for bats and birds and bugs of all kinds. The dirt
bikes are controlled, the illegal dumping is finally put to an
end, and there are even sites for camping in the Meadowlands.

"It would be a unique experience," Smith says, imagining it.
"The backdrop for your campfire is the New York City skyline." This may not be the vision that everyone at the HMDC
has in mind—you only have to spend a few minutes in the
lobby to hear guys talking more like real estate agents than
land stewards—but for a decade now these kinds of things
have been happening. On one side of Mount Arlington, rap-
tors use the thermal draft rising up the side of the garbage hill
to coast until they make their dive. "If he comes down in
phragmites, a hawk will break a wing. And look over there.
That's a freshwater pond on top of this hill. We've seen
muskrats in there, painted turtles, and we're two hundred feet
up!" He added, "You know, we had biologists up here and
they said, 'Nobody's doing grassland habitat on this scale in
the country.' But, of course, not to dwell on it, but you have
people like Bill Sheehan, who can't say anything positive
about us. I mean, if I had it in my power to restore the Meadowlands to what it was three hundred years ago—as interesting as that would be and as much as I would like to walk
through a cedar forest here—that land would not be as
important to society as what we're doing with this land
today." In the long run, Smith holds up his quarrels with
Sheehan as proof of how difficult it is to get anything done in
the Meadowlands at all.

After a while, we drove back to the headquarters of the
HMDC, which is known as the Environment Center. There is
a nature trail decorated with an array of native plant species
that runs up alongside an old dump. There is a wildlife exhibit
and a little garbage museum for the kids. The HMDC even
rents out a conference room on the Kingsland Marsh for weddings. The flyer advertising the weddings says, "You have
dreamed of this event since you were a little girl. Imagine

yourself in a glass-enclosed gazebo, resting serenely on the water, with a breathtaking view of the Manhattan skyline, and embraced by the elegance of nature—a guaranteed perfect setting for the most romantic day of your life." The flyer doesn't mention the area is all built on old construction spoils, on slave lands, dumps, and perhaps what's left of a missing body or two. The Hackensack Meadowlands Development Commission's Environment Center focuses on the future. On the way back with Don Smith, I was wondering about the past. A long while back I'd read about a plan to replant the Atlantic white cedar. I had seen newspaper clippings of Smith, in 1985, and an HMDC landscape architect planting Atlantic cedar seedlings in the Kearny Marsh. Smith had long hair then and looked geeky. At the time, the executive director of the HMDC was quoted as saying, "We want to have at least one section of the region where a visitor can get the feel of the great primeval forests which once covered North America." I asked Smith whatever happened to those trees, three hundred of them, each four feet tall, and grouped in four small strands. "They died," Smith said. "Yeah, and that was me and another guy lugging all those trees across the marsh in a canoe. There was a big storm in December of ninety-two that brought salt water into the marsh. It may be that the Atlantic cedar just won't grow in this area anymore. Things have changed so much. But we're working on something else that might work in there instead."

Point-No-Point

OH, MEADOWLANDS, WHAT WILL BECOME OF YOU IF YOUR reeds eventually lift you up and dry you and shake off your remaining swampness and transform you into yet another kind of meadow? (And what will we call you then?) What new industries will one day rise up from your waste-laced soils and smear your already smeared landscape and write on you once more, progress's palimpsest, technology's Etch-A-Sketch? How many people will look at you some day and write up a memo or organize a commission or hire someone to write a prospectus and say that you could be something else, something more, something much better with new and improved features for everyone to enjoy, even the kids? How many more people, oh, Meadowlands, will be tossed into your streams, hidden dead in your fields—which are not so much fields as layers of what was no longer wanted by anybody? How many more of those dead, long dead, and long-decayed people who have been sent to you, who have been taken for a ride, will settle down, down to that place deep in the peat and past the clay and beyond the age-old mud, down to where your rivers all run dry? And how is it that you will still somehow manage to be spoiled but unspoiled, trod upon and bulldozed, remediated and reclaimed, dumped in and sprayed all over but somehow never spent?

These are the kinds of things I was thinking about one rainy winter day as as I drove to Point-No-Point to wander around alone beneath the Pulaski Skyway. I never know for certain where I am when I am in Point-No-Point without a guide, and on that day I began to feel particularly lost because it was raining a lot and I felt as if I was caught in a herd of trucks as they ran for the old truck bridge and because my windshield was all fogged up. I crossed and recrossed the old truck bridge and while doing so I felt a little jumpy thinking I was going to be hit. Pretty soon, I got out of there and, without really thinking about it, ended up heading south along the eastern shore of Newark Bay, to Bayonne. I knew this place to have been meadows, meadows and beaches where people swam and vacationed. Once, Bayonne was called the Newport of New York, but then oil refineries puffed smoke onto its beaches and industry came, and the old hotels were abandoned and torn down and New Yorkers vacationed elsewhere. Now I saw mostly old piers and crumbling concrete, with a few new housing developments thrown in. I had never been so far down on this shore of Newark Bay before and I looked out across the slate gray water and saw the stacks of the oil refineries that cough up smoke and spit out flames.

As a rule, I don't generally venture below Point-No-Point. For reasons I'm not certain about, I feel gloomy when I'm too far south in the Meadowlands. On the coast of old Bayonne or in the junkyards that are on the Newark side of the sealike Newark Bay, I can't seem to find a way in anywhere. I can't get up the nerve to plunge into the particular breed of junkyard that grows there, through the particular kind of rubble, through the particular fields of weeds. The Meadowlands are just too *concentrated* beyond Point-No-Point. And if I can't find a way in, then I might not find a way out: chaos rules. I'll take a mosquito ditch on the Carlstadt Meadows or a landfill in Secaucus over anything along Newark Bay. Especially in the abstract, the bottom of the Meadowlands scares me. Still, on this particular trip, the rain stopped as I drove, and I thought the sun might even break through the cold, sad sky, so for the moment I was okay.

When I got to the very tip of Bayonne, to the bottom of the Meadowlands, to the farthest point down I had ever been, I was afraid I would be overwhelmed again: underneath the bridge were washed-out industrial flats and a lonely stretch of the Kill van Kull, a Dutch-named channel that cuts between Staten Island and New Jersey and creeps out to New York Harbor. But then, I spotted a little park, a jewel of manicured green, and I parked my car and walked into it. There, I saw a man who was watching his granddaughter play on the swings and run along the water's edge. He waved at me and smiled so I approached him and we talked for a while about how wonderful Bayonne had once been and about the factory he used to work in before it was demolished. In a few minutes, the granddaughter ran off and the grandfather waved good-bye to me and slowly followed the child. I was feeling about as upbeat as I figured I could feel about this section of the old meadows, so I decided to get in my car and head back north to the dumps and the Skyway when I realized I had lost my keys. A policeman I hadn't seen immediately signaled me from across the parking lot—he had watched me drop my keys and was holding them for me. I thanked him profusely and he was cordial and polite and I was again about to leave with good feelings for this area when an old man motioned for me from his car. I walked to him, reluctantly, and he said, "You're friends with Tommy, huh?" He was talking about the police-man. I said, no, not really and tried to explain, but he cut me off. "Here," he said. He held out a tattered copy of an old *Reader's Digest*. "Take these articles," he said. "I wrote in them. Go ahead. Tommy knows." He nodded toward the policeman, who was by now driving away. I took the magazine and quickly got in my car and drove back up to Point-No-Point. I forgot all about the man's old magazine until a few days later, when I was turning in my car at the rental place and I found it in the backseat. When I paged through, I saw that he had underlined the gory details of several murders mentioned in one of the articles in the magazine. At that point, I put it away and scolded myself for ever having ventured down that far in the Meadowlands. I probably won't go down there ever again.

Notes

SNAKE HILL

p. 13   The bus route described is that of New Jersey Transit Bus Number
         190, though many other commuter buses offer similarly spectacular
         views of the Meadowlands.

p. 16   Sources for the geological history of the Meadowlands include *The
         Geology and Landscapes of New Jersey; The Geology and Geography of New
         Jersey,* by Kemble Widmer; and an unpublished report written by
         Kevin W. Wright and commissioned by the Hackensack Meadow-
         lands Development Commission Environment Center. Wright's
         report was used as background for a display of historical materials
         that is today at the Hackensack Meadowlands Development Com-
         mission Environment Center in Lyndhurst, New Jersey.

p. 17   *The New York Times* editorial about the Meadowlands, "Requiem
         for the Meadows," ran on March 25, 1959.

p. 17   *The New York Times* article describing new developments in the
         Meadowlands ran on June 29, 1987.

pp. 18–20   Union City is the most densely populated city in New Jersey, which is the most densely populated state in the United States. According to *The Times,* December 3, 1995, sixty thousand people live in the city's 1.27 square miles. The smells smelled when passing over the New Jersey Turnpike bridge and over the Pulaski Skyway were identified for me by Pam Shipley, who as an art student in New York City, often rode from the city to New Jersey on a motorcycle. Leonid Brezhnev's experiences in the Meadowlands have been related to me on so many occasions by so many people that I suspect they are lore, but I once read the same story in a political journal. Tom Hanlon, a film historian in Fort Lee, told me that the Meadowlands were used as a stand-in for the western prairie by the early motion picture industry. The story of the man starting out across the meadows in the fall and being discovered dead the next spring was reported in *The Star-Ledger* in a series of articles written about the Meadowlands in 1959 by John T. Cunningham, a newspaperman and historian. Cunningham has written so many books about New Jersey that bits of his writing and reporting seem to have made their way into all subsequent writings about New Jersey like strands of primordial DNA. One of the landscape painters who painted the Meadowlands was Martin Johnson Heade—see *Jersey Meadows,* which hangs at the Smith College Museum of Art in Northampton, Massachusetts. That TV cameramen use the Meadowlands for nature shots was told to me by a TV cameraman named Robert Sullivan.

pp. 20–26   Information about Secaucus came from a number of sources, including: "History of Snake Hill," by Nicholas Facciolla, in *Meadowlands/USA* magazine, which is published by the Meadowlands Chamber of Commerce (I found an undated photocopy of this article in the Secaucus Library); "Minerals of Snake Hill," also by Nicholas Facciolla, a pamphlet. Secaucus's reputation as a national joke is explained in *History of Secaucus, New Jersey: Emphasizing Its Earlier Development,* a report kept in a loose-leaf binder in the Secaucus Library. The book further states: "Although the town of Secaucus has never been the site of any particular event, historical or otherwise, travelling Secaucusites will find it known by many a person as far west as Chicago and men returning from war tell stories of its 'fame' even beyond." Also, Paul Amico, who was mayor of Secaucus for many years, keeps a series of clips regarding Secaucus's reputation in his basement.

AN ACHIEVEMENT OF THE FUTURE

pp. 36–38   The names of the Lenape Indians' sachems and other information about the Hackensacks came from Wright's HMDC report and from Peter O. Wacker's *Land & People: A Cultural Geography of Preindustrial New Jersey.* I found Lenape words in A *Lenâpé-English Dictionary,* an anonymous manuscript found in the archives of the Moravian Church in Bethlehem, Pennsylvania. The dictionary was published in 1889 by the Historical Society of Pennsylvania as part of the Pennsylvanian Student Series and edited by Daniel G. Brinton, professor of American Archaeology and Linguistics at the University of Pennsylvania, and Reverend Albert Seqaqkind Anthony, assistant missionary to the Delawares and Six Nations, Canada. I read descriptions of salt hay farming in numerous old newspaper articles and from Cunningham's Meadowlands series. The history of the salt marshes and salt marsh grasses came from Wacker and from *From Marsh to Farm: The Landscape Transformation of Coastal New Jersey,* by Kimberly R. Sebold. The description of Newark residents as unscrupulous came from *The Kearny Observer* of January 18, 1908. A beautiful book about East Coast salt marshes in general is *Life and Death of the Salt Marsh,* by John and Mildred Teal, published in 1969. To get an idea of what the Meadowlands once looked like, take a trip down the Garden State Parkway in New Jersey. Take the Route 9 exit and follow Route 9 southwest to Route 542. Then take Route 542 to Route 563 and as you cross the bridge over the river look up the Mullica River valley.

pp. 37–39   I found descriptions of animal life long ago in the Meadowlands in Wright, in Cunningham, and in a *New Yorker* article written about the Meadowlands in 1957 by John Brooks. Brooks wrote before the Meadowlands Sports Complex was built so that, in many ways, it is about a Meadowlands that no longer exists. Still, it's one of the best articles ever written about the Meadowlands. (Brooks said that he used to dream about the salt marsh grasses as a giant inland sea.) Daniel Van Winkle wrote about hunting, fishing, and cattail stripping in *The History of Hudson County, New Jersey*, published in 1924.

pp. 39–40   The cedar forests are described in Wacker, in Brooks, in Cunningham, and in old newspaper stories about the Meadowlands that I found in the Kearny Library and in the Newark Library. The fact that the Continental Army floated logs cut in the Meadowlands came from *The Journal of Isaac Bangs: April 1 to July 29, 1776*. Bangs visited the home of Colonel John Schuyler, and in his journal, he reports on the meadows, on the Schuylers, and on getting really drunk. The fact that a New Jersey Turnpike Commissioner wanted to take the stumps out of the Kearny Marsh was told to me by several people at the Hackensack Meadowlands Development Commission. Sometimes, when I was exploring in the libraries around the edges of the Meadowlands, it seemed that any old paper I picked up had notes of interest about the old meadows. In 1901, for instance, *The Newark Sunday News* published a report on the wild animal farm in the Newark meadows. As it turned out, the Meadowlands were once a stop for animals that were coming into the country and on their way to zoos: "The savage roaring of lions and tigers, the fierce growl of angry bears, the bellowing of elephants, the snarling of hyenas and wolves—these are some of the sounds occasionally wafted across the meadows towards Newark by an easterly wind."

pp. 41–43   The early history of the Schuyler mine is recounted in *A Place in History: North Arlington, New Jersey: A Centennial Chronicle of the Birthplace of Steam Power in America*, by Merritt Ierley, a book published in 1996. The introduction to this book was written by William E. Worthington, specialist in steam power at the Smithsonian Institute. He wrote, "The importance of Schuyler's steam engine lay not just in the fact that it was the first in America: more significantly, it was the harbinger of an event unlike any other in history." And he goes on about it being the beginning of a "new age." "It would be the era of an industrial revolution," he said. Worthington asks, "Who, in March 1755, could have possibly imagined the significance of the event about to take place at Colonel John Schuyler's North Arlington copper mine?" Additional information about the mine came from *The Newark Sunday Call, The Newark Evening News,*

The Star-Ledger, and *The Old Copper Mines of New Jersey,* by Harry B. Weiss and Grace M. Weiss. There are numerous maps of the North Arlington Mine in the North Arlington Public Library. Descriptions of the events around the time of the cave-ins were published in *The North Arlington Leader* and *The New York Times.* I am grateful to Donald E. DeRogatis, construction official for the borough of North Arlington, for explaining how the mine shaft cave-ins were handled by the borough and the state.

pp. 43–48   Sources for details about the industrial history of Newark include such books as *Made in New Jersey: The Industrial Story of a State,* by John T. Cunningham; *Newark,* by Cunningham; *The Research State: A History of Science in New Jersey,* by John R. Pierce and Arthur G. Tressler; and *New Jersey: History of Ingenuity and Industry,* by James P. Johnson. Information about Thomas Cort came from the first volume of the three-volume *Biographical and Geneological History of Newark and Essex County, New Jersey,* which was published in 1898. Seth Boyden was the subject of a number of pamphlets and old magazine articles that I read at the Newark Library. Also, there were a lot of stories about him in the Newark press around the time of his death. I found additional information about Boyden and about Newark's industrial history in *Newark: America's Unhealthiest City, 1832–1895,* by Stuart Galishoff, and in *The Newarker,* which called itself "The House Organ of the Newark Free Public Library." Galishoff's book is excellent on the introduction of sewers in Newark, where citizens at that time made their way through streets filled with all manner of waste. Galishoff explains that the British sanitary reformer, Sir Edwin Chadwick, recommended the use of small, egg-shaped sewer pipes to loosen solids so that even bricks and rats could flow easily down into, in Newark's case, the Passaic River and the meadows. At one time, the various industrial smells of Newark could have inspired an entire set of Crayola Color 'n' Smell crayons: according to the April 1914 issue of *The Newarker,* "The Newark odor is composite. Through the vaulted chambers of our Library, as the fickle wind veers, come, wave after wave, the banana-peel odor from bleacheries, pungent flavor of acid-makers, yeasty whiffs from bakeries, the camphor-laden aroma of celluloid, the clinging breath of dried tobacco, cloying steam from the candy-maker, clean hospital odors from disinfectants, the oily smell of grease-makers, the heavy odor of paint factories, the disgust-provoking redolence from soap-makers, the bitter flavor of bruised hops from breweries, and finally the strong-bodied smells from seventy-seven tanneries—not to mention the odor of sanctity from the semi-circle of church towers which guard us round about."

pp. 49–56   Samuel Pike, S. B. Driggs, and the Swartwouts are all described in Brooks's 1957 article and in numerous articles about the meadows by Cunningham. Charles McGillycuddy wrote of the Jersey meadows in an article entitled "An Achievement of the Future," published in *The Quaker* in 1899. C. C. Vermeule is quoted in "Drainage of the Hackensack and Newark Tide-Marshes," in *New Jersey Geological Survey,* the annual report, 1896. The two Dutch engineers were reported on in *The New York Times* on March 20, 1959. Additional information about Driggs's iron dikes came from *Frank Leslie's Illustrated Newspaper,* November 16, 1867; from *The New York Times,* March 18, 1871; and from the 1867 prospectus of the Iron Dike and Land Reclamation Company of New York, which was entitled, "Facts concerning the Reclamation of Swamp and Marsh Lands and the Strengthening of River Levees and Banks of Canals & c., & c., by Means of An Iron Dike," and which was found for me, as many of these books were, by the interlibrary loan department at central branch of the Multnomah County Library in Portland, Oregon. I learned that Richard Riker was once a New York City mayoral candidate in *The Encyclopedia of New York,* edited by Kenneth T. Jackson. I read Robert Swartwout's papers in the Manuscripts Archives Division of the New York Public Library. The Swartwouts are also mentioned in *The Swartwout Chronicles,* a family history of the Swartwouts, also found in the New York Public Library, and in *The Great American Land Bubble,* by A. Sakolski.

GONE WITH THE WIND

p. 58   Information on the explosions that occurred near the Days Inn that I stayed at came from the September 4, 1995, editions of *The Star-Ledger* and *The Bergen Record.*

pp. 65–68   Information about Philip Kearny came from many sources,

Notes

including *Letters from the Peninsula: The Civil War Letters of General Philip Kearny,* by William B. Styple, and an article about General Kearny by Arthur F. Lenehan that I found in the Kearny Library pamphlet files.

p. 69   The history of Kearny soccer was explained to me by members of The Thistle, Kearny's famous youth soccer league, and by Charles Waller and George Rogers, the curators of the Kearny Library's July 1996 Olympic athlete memorabilia display. (Eleven Kearny athletes have been to the Olympics, and two Kearny residents were on the U.S. Olympic rowing team that summer.) I am also indebted to Mr. Waller, one of Kearny's historians, and to Mr. Rogers for giving me a tour of the Kearny History Museum at a time when the museum was closed to the public for renovations.

pp. 71–72   Margaret Mitchell's relationship with her book, *Gone with the Wind,* is discussed in *Margaret Mitchell's Gone with the Wind Letters, 1936–1949,* edited by Richard Harwell. Mitchell wrote of the French translation of *Gone with the Wind:* "I have found that a number of our good Southern idioms had suffered delightful sea changes. I was especially amused when Gerald O'Hara ejaculated 'oo, la la.' "

WALDEN SWAMP

pp. 78–90   On our trips across the Meadowlands, we referred to U.S. Geological Survey maps of the area, and to Rand McNally's *Streetmap of Hudson County.* To find out where the cedar forests were, I referred to a map drawn especially for C. C. Vermeule, and published in 1866 alongside his article, "Drainage of the Hackensack and Newark Tide-Marshes." At the end of our explorations, Dave drew a map (see Frontispiece).

pp. 85–88   Details about the mercury dump in the Meadowlands were reported in *The Star-Ledger* and in an article in the February 11, 1979, edition of *The Passaic Herald-News. The Sporting News* ran an article about the possible ill effects of playing football in the Meadowlands Sports Complex on September 7, 1987. Don Smith of the Hackensack Meadowlands Development Commission identified the ducks Dave and I saw as Muscovy ducks when I sent him pic-

213

Notes

tures of the birds. His postcard to me said in part: "Excellent meat birds, wild cousins live in Central and Northern S. America."

VALLEY OF THE GARBAGE HILLS

pp. 93–94   Most of the information in this chapter was drawn from conversations with dump workers and state and municipal officials associated in one way or another with the Meadowlands dumps, but two articles were especially helpful with the history of garbage dumping in the Meadowlands, and they were published in *The Bergen Record* of July 9, 1995 ("Reclaiming the Meadows; Natural Habitat Is Scarred and Stressed") and in *The Star-Ledger,* February 9, 1976. The story of the Keegan landfill and the Lend-Lease Act was told to me by the dump owner's son, John Keegan. I also read that, in 1922, Kearny had a poppy problem. The poppies came from France, where they grew on war graves. They were imported to America as seeds hidden in a ship's ballast. For a few years, the dumps in Kearny were covered with fields of red.

p. 97   I am grateful to Professor Robert Hamm, professor of civil and environmental engineering at the University of Wisconsin, for speaking with me about the microscopic organisms that live in landfills.

p. 97   The ingredients of leachate came from a Meadowlands leachate analysis shared with me by Chris Dour of the HMDC.

SKEETERS

pp. 107–8   Historical information about mosquitoes in the meadows came from a pamphlet published circa 1938 by the Federal Writers' Project that was called *Stories of New Jersey* (the particular story in the pamphlet was titled "The Mosquito War"); from *The Newark News,* April 29, 1926; *The Newark News,* April 1945; and from Cunningham's *Star-Ledger* Meadowlands series. The bursting mosquito was described by Henry Wanset, a British visitor to the Meadowlands, quoted in *The Newark Sunday News,* July 11, 1948.

pp. 108–14   I read about John B. Smith in numerous folders of clippings and speeches and obituaries in the archives at Rutgers University in New Brunswick. I also read numerous articles that Smith published on The Mosquito War. A good place to learn more about the history of mosquito control is *The Path Between the Seas,* David McCullough's book on the making of the Panama Canal, in which I found the information regarding Dr. Albert Freeman Africanus King, Walter Reed and yellow fever, and about malaria epidemics in the United States. I am grateful for conversations I had with Leland Merrill, retired dean of the Agricultural School at Rutgers; he mailed me an unpublished paper that he wrote on Smith. Also helpful was "The Works of Professor John B. Smith in Economic Entomology," an article in *The Staten Island Association of Arts and Sciences* (October 1911 to May 1912), by E. L. Dickerson. Smith wrote hundreds of scientific articles himself, with titles such as "Notes on Some Experiments with a House Fly," "Is the Woodpecker Useful?," and "Remedy for Onion Maggot."

p. 115   Leonard Soccio was promoted from chief inspector to director of the Bergen County Mosquito Control Commission since the time I first spoke with him.

p. 117   I read about how mosquitoes draw blood in several places, including *Mosquitoes,* by J. D. Gillett. Gillett also writes interestingly about mosquito swarming, which is little understood. Mosquito swarms are usually same sex, like old-time social clubs—although, Gillett writes, "a female may fly into a male swarm whereupon she is seized by one of the dancing males and the pair drops out to continue in private."

p. 123   Victor spent some time hoping to find an Asian tiger mosquito; however, none have been found in northern New Jersey. The tiger mosquito, a mosquito that is thought to have arrived in America from Asia inside used tires, is the latest mosquito threat in southern New Jersey. I recently read an article in the September 1997 issue of *Outside,* that said that Asian tiger mosquitoes were suspected in the outbreak of LaCrosse encephalitis—though nothing has been pinned on them yet. And while I was in the Meadowlands with the Mosquitoes Commission employees, encephalitis outbreaks were occurring in Connecticut, thanks to mosquitoes. Malaria-carrying mosquitoes are by no means eradicated worldwide. According to *The New York Times,* January 8, 1997, "Between 300 million and 500 million people now get malaria each year, and someone dies of it every fifteen seconds—mostly children and pregnant women."

Notes

TREASURE

pp. 130–32   The particular letters of Leo Koncher's that I selected were all originally published in *The Star-Ledger*.

pp. 132–34   The account of the pirate battle and description of the pirates who operated in New York Harbor was drawn mainly from Daniel Van Winkle's *History of Hudson County*.

DIGGING

p. 143   Although I concentrated on the PJP landfill as a Hoffa digging site, Giants Stadium still remains the most discussed possible site for Hoffa—it seems that every time I turn on ESPN and there is a game being played at the Meadowlands, I hear some crack about Hoffa—and I have a backup plan for investigating it one day. New Jersey was the home of the motion picture business from the late 1880s until the 1920s before it moved to Hollywood; Newark and Fort Lee and Bayonne were home to many studios, and once, while I was speaking with Tom Hanlon, the film historian in Fort Lee, about the history of filmmaking in the Meadowlands, he mentioned he had been in the film business himself, and shortly after the invention of an early form of video, he took a video camera to the East Rutherford dumps where Giants Stadium was being built. He filmed a lot of the construction of Giants Stadium. He still has the videotape, though he never reviewed it in its entirety because it would mean changing the video format to make it modern and that would be a big hassle. "I've always wondered if maybe I have Hoffa on there, though," he said to me. (He also said to me that he was the one who came up with the idea to run a water pipe across the George Washington Bridge to New York City when in the early 1970s the city was suffering from a severe drought and ended up drinking New Jersey water. "I knew one of the water engineers in New Jersey," he said, "so as soon as I thought of it I gave him a call.")

p. 146   The contents of the PJP Landfill are described in numerous state reports that I read in the New Jersey Room of the Jersey City Library. There are plans afoot to build a ball field on the old dump.

pp. 143–48   Information about Jimmy Hoffa's disappearance came from

216

New York Times reports that ran through the fall and winter of 1975, just after he vanished, at a time when possible Hoffa burial sites were springing up all over the country—in a dump in Arizona, in a Detroit trucking terminal, and, according to a guy who convinced the news department at CBS to pay him $10,000 for Hoffa's whereabouts, in a cement tomb off the coast of Florida (the guy took off with the money and, of course, they didn't find Hoffa in Florida). Additional information about Hoffa's disappearance is also discussed in *Desperate Bargain: Why Jimmy Hoffa Had to Die,* by Lester Velie; in *Hoffa,* by Arthur Sloane; and in *The Teamsters,* by Steve Brill. Brill's book contains chapters on both Hoffa and Anthony Provenzano. In the Provenzano chapter, the elevator operator takes Brill up to the offices, where Brill manages somehow to have a sit-down with Salvatore "Sammy" Provenzano, Tony Pro's brother, in which Sammy says things like, "I try to mind my own business. . . . I don't want no trouble. . . . I'm just here to get the job done. . . ." At the end of Sloane's book, the reader is given an opportunity to choose a Hoffa disappearance theory: that Hoffa was killed by the Mob by accident; that the Mob had nothing to do with Hoffa's death at all; that the Mob killed him on purpose because he was in the way of its relationship with the Teamsters. Sloane also mentions other people who are possibly buried in the PJP landfill, such as Armand "Cookie" Faugno, an alleged loan shark who allegedly rubbed Tony Provenzano the wrong way, and Anthony Castellito, a union competitor of Provenzano's who may have picked the wrong guy to compete with (neither person's body was ever found). A former member of Provenzano's union talked to me about Provenzano, but I promised I wouldn't mention his name.

p. 153   Katherine Weidel, senior landscape architect at the HMDC, identified the British soldier lichen that I discovered on the PJP landfill.

p. 153   My digging was sponsored in part by Geoquest, Inc., a treasure hunting store in Saddle Brook, New Jersey. I went to Geoquest hoping to rent metal detectors, but when I told Laola and Harry Nicholas, the husband and wife proprietors, what I was doing, we began talking, first, about the FBI human remains detection seminar that the husband had attended (apparently, dumped bodies can often be found with metal detectors if the body dumped has a lot of

Notes

dental fillings in it or jewelry on it), and, second, about aerial treasure hunting devices I might use (which were out of my budget). In the end, they wouldn't let me pay for my use of their metal detectors. I spent a lot of time looking at the treasure hunting guidebooks to various parts of the country. Treasure hunting guidebooks are like regular guidebooks except that in every picture of, say, a scenic sunset there is a man or a woman in the corner listening intently to his or her metal detector.

Other digging sponsors I would like to acknowledge are Gillian Blake, Nan Graham, Kris Dahl, M. B. Sharpe, Gerald Marzorati, Mia Di Iorio, Tobias Perse, S. McPherson, Louise Grace, and Samuel Emmet.

pp. 153–62   I received permission to dig in the Keegan landfill for remnants of London from John Keegan. Among the reasons we dug in the area that we dug in were my conversations with Tom Marturano, director of solid waste and engineering at the HMDC. Marturano looked over old aerial photographs with me. As it turned out, he too has dreamed of digging for London. We talked about digging up Penn Station. But in the midst of our conversations, I found some pillars. When I did, I stopped talking to him about the buried Penn Station because I wanted to be on record as being the first to rediscover Penn Station in the modern era. Still, because he helped me, I was trying to give him hints about where the pillars might be, though I'm sure he thought I was being really weird. For the most part, I just clammed up. Later, it turned out that Don Smith, the HMDC naturalist, remembered Penn Station pillars being buried beneath the HMDC headquarters, as landfill. Also, Dave found an eagle from Penn Station in an antique store while walking around one afternoon in Manhattan.

The exterior of Penn Station was modeled on the wall of columns that surrounds the Piazza of St. Peter's in Rome, which was originally designed by Giovanni Bernini.

BODIES

pp. 172–78   Information on early roads and transportation in New Jersey came from the book *From Indian Trail to Iron Horse: Travel and*

Transportation in New Jersey, by Wheaton J. Lane. Train facts came from a series of articles written about New Jersey railroads by John T. Cunningham and originally published in *The Newark Sunday News* magazine in 1951 and then republished as a book entitled *Railroading in New Jersey.* When the Pulaski Skyway opened, newspapers all over the New York metropolitan area went on about how much time the trip saved. I read articles in *The Newark News, The Star-Ledger, The New York Times,* and the *Herald Tribune.* Most papers wrote editorials about how great the Skyway was and how great the meadows soon would be because of the Skyway. For instance, *The Times* wrote, "The day is no doubt coming when the mosquito-infested jungle of rank vegetation will be only a memory of the oldest inhabitants of Secaucus and Kearny." A recent *New York Times* article written about the Skyway that was helpful was headlined AT 60, THE PULASKI SKYWAY DRAWS ADMIRATION AND CRITICISM and was published on October 10, 1993. Jack Friedenrich, a former chief bridge engineer for the state of New Jersey, recollected working under Sven Hedin, the Skyway engineer who, after his work on the Skyway, preceded Friedenrich as state bridge engineer. I had help with the vehicle miles saved (VMS) figures from Eric Etheridge, a Skyway enthusiast.

pp. 174–77   I read about Frank Hague in *The Boss: The Hague Machine in Action,* by Dayton David McKean, and in a profile written of Hague by John McCarten and published in two parts in *The New Yorker* in 1938; also in an unpublished paper on Hague written by Charles Markey and stored in the New Jersey History Room of the Jersey City Library. One of the best hagiographies about Hague is entitled *The Greatest Mayor That Ever Lived,* by John J. Corcoran, Jr., and published in 1981. I read the details of The War on the Meadows in the *Jersey City Journal* articles that ran nearly every day during the winter of 1931 to 1932.

pp. 178–79   I found numerous pamphlets on the life of Casimir Pulaski in the Jersey City Library, many of them written for the ceremony held upon the dedication of the Skyway in his name on October 11, 1933.

pp. 180–82   Additional information about the Nicole DeCombe murder came from stories in *The New York Times* and *The Bergen Record,* from

stories by United Press International, and from my conversations
with the Hudson County Prosecutor's office.

The Trapper and the Fisherman

p. 185   Since the time that Don Smith and Bill Sheehan sat down to
lunch, Bill Sheehan's group HEART has changed its name to Hackensack Riverkeeper, Inc. Also in that time, Smith and Sheehan have
appeared together at several river-oriented events. As far as I know,
no one has gotten hurt.

About the Author

Robert Sullivan has written for *The New York Times Magazine, The New Yorker, The New Republic, Rolling Stone, Outside, Condé Nast Traveler,* and *Vogue,* where he is a contributing editor. He lives in Portland, Oregon, with his wife and two children.